BR STE. MOTIVE P DEPO'

C000260136

W R

Paul Bolger

Nottingham

Booklaw Publications

Preface

The purpose of this book is to assist the average enthusiast be he modeller, relic collector or historian, with his search for information on Motive Power Depots — the home of the steam locomotive.

Many devotees will recall the experience of touring such an establishment; the hiss of steam, the clank of engine movements and the sight of smoke suspended from the ceilings above the many varieties of engine in different stages of repair.

The sight of a fully serviced locomotive simmering outside the depot on a crisp bright morning is a memory I shall never forget. I hope that the following pages aid the reminiscences of those fortunate enough to have lived during the steam age.

This book is dedicated to Bill Potter, whose prolonged help with photographs greatly assisted the compilation of these books.

Paul Bolger

Front cover, top: *A trio of '51xx' 2-6-2Ts and a 'County' at Newton Abbot in June 1960. Left to right Nos 5158, 4105, 5164 (all 83A) and 1016* County of Hants *(84G).* P. H. Groom

Front cover, bottom: *The southern entrance of the three-road shed at Worcester in 1964 with 'Castle' 4-6-0 No 7025* Sudeley Castle *(minus nameplates) in the foreground. This locomotive was withdrawn from 85A in September of that year.* W. Potter

Back cover, top: *The interior of Swindon a month before closure in October 1964.* N. E. Preedy

Back cover, centre: *A close-up of ex-Rhymney Railway 0-6-0Ts Nos 72 and 39 at Cardiff East Dock in 1951 (both 88B), No 72 was withdrawn in February 1952, but No 39 survived until August 1955.* Real Photos

Back cover, bottom: *The western end of Machynlleth, on 23 June 1958 with Class 2251 0-6-0 No 2251 sporting a 'Cambrian Coast Express' headboard.* W. Potter

First published 1983

This edition published by
Book Law Publications 2009

Printed and Bound by
The Amadeus Press, Cleckheaton, BD19 4TQ.

Introduction

For reasons of parity with the previous volumes — *BR Steam Motive Power Depots LMR, ER, ScR and SR* (all Ian Allan) — the depots covered by this work have been restricted to those which possessed a code, as these were the most visited and of greater importance to the railway network.

In all, 63 depots are outlined. For continuity of the text the codes used as headings are c1950.

Acknowledgements

This book has been made possible with the invaluable help of the following people and organisations: Mr R. J. Collins and Mr W. F. C. Phillips of Bristol Divisional Civil Engineers Dept, British Rail; Mr Winch and Mr Fairclough of Cambridge University Library; Mr G. M. Kichenside of Locomotive and General Railway Photographs; Miss S. Percy of the Ordnance Survey; Mr C. Turner of Photomatic; Mr D. Wood of the Worcester Locomotive Society.

In addition, special thanks are extended to the following: D. H. Cape, R. S. Carpenter; D. Carville; H. C. Casserley; P. G. Cooper; A. G. Ellis; K. Fairey; D. Fish; R. A. Garland; B. K. B. Green; P. H. Groom; M. Hale; P. Hawkins; B. Hilton; M. S. Houlgrave; J. Koefoed; F. Lyon; E. Lyons; B. Morrison; T. W. Nicholls; C. H. S. Owen; J. A. Peden; W. Potter; N. E. Preedy; D. Rendell; R. C. Riley; G. F. Roose; G. W. Sharpe; J. L. Stevenson; W. T. Stubbs; A. A. Vickers; A. Warrington; T. Wright.

In the course of preparation the following publications were of major importance as reference and consultative material:

The Railway Observer (Volumes 18 to 38)
The Railway Magazine (Volumes 94 to 114)
The Railway World (Volumes 19 to 29)
Trains Illustrated & Modern Railways (Volumes 3 to 21)

Notes about Contents

The depots at Bath Green Park and Templecombe have not been included as they were of SDJR origin and did not become Western Region property until 1958. They are within the Southern Region volume as 71G and 71H respectively. Of the two GWR/LNWR joint sheds, Birkenhead and Shrewsbury, the former has been catered for in the LMR book as 6C because of complete LMR control from 1951. The WR took charge of Shrewsbury in 1949 and is thus included as 84G. Swansea Victoria, Abergavenny and Tredegar are within the LMR volume as 4B, 4D and 4E respectively, as all were of LNWR origin and retained their LMS identities until 1949. Bromsgrove, Bristol Barrow Road and Gloucester Barnwood are also within the LMR book (21C, 22A, 22B) because their pedigree was ex-Midland Railway and all were LMR controlled until WR takeover in 1958. The ex-GCR shed at Wrexham Rhosddu follows the same rule and is catalogued as 6E in the LMR volume.

The ex-LSWR sheds, Exmouth Junction, Yeovil Town, Plymouth Friary, Barnstaple Junction and Wadebridge are all within the SR book as 72A, 72C, 72D, 72E and 72F respectively. They did not become

2

WR property until 1962, except Plymouth Friary which succumbed in 1958.

It must be remembered that strict compliance with the coding system would have resulted in severe duplication of the contents of most volumes and no less the WR for the reasons given above. A balance has been necessary to combat the regional boundary changes and BR's failure to issue each region with its codes in January 1948. It is hoped that the resulting regional 'limbo' where it occurs will not hinder your enjoyment of the book.

Pre-Grouping Origins

Although, primarily, not relevant to the period covered, an indication of the vintage of the shed is given by the inclusion of the company of ownership prior to 1923. This is not necessarily the company which commissioned the building, as many smaller installations were absorbed into the larger companies by the takeover or amalgamation of district railways.

Gazetteer References

These numbers refer to the page and square within the Ian Allan Pre-Grouping Atlas which pinpoint the subject's national location.

Closing Dates

The dates given indicate the closure of the depot to steam engines only. However, in some cases the date would have been the same for diesels where the building closed completely, either as a result of its dilapidated condition or the effects of the 'Beeching' cuts.

Shed-Codes

The Western Region was not issued with shed-codes at the outset of nationalisation in 1948 owing to BR's indecision over districts. In 1949 it was allocated ex-LMS type codes commencing with 81A. A full list of all codes is given on page 127.

Allocations

Where the depot's lifetime allows, three separate allocations, of steam locomotives only, are listed from the years 1950, 1959 and 1965. These lists are accurate in August 1950, March 1959 and May 1965.

Very few sets of allocations are in absolute numerical order as preference has been given to listing the locos in classification groups to keep this book on a par with previous volumes. The Western Region numbering system was a continuance of the GWR method and batches of numbers for one class of engine were often a thousand digits distant from each other (ie the 'Hall' class were represented by the prefixes 49, 59, 69 and 79. In most cases different classes did not share the same prefix and could thus be identified easier. The resulting lists are as consecutive as this 'leap-frogging' of classes will allow.

Plans

All the plans have been based upon the Ordnance Survey County and National Grid series maps from various years and reproduction is by permission of the Controller of Her Majesty's Stationery Office, Crown Copyright Reserved.

Photographs

All except four of the 105 illustrations have been restricted to the period 1948/67. The majority of the views are hitherto unpublished and represent many years of search.

Newport Pill shed in June 1958 with two of its workforce of '57xx' 0-6-0PT and '42xx' 2-8-0T classes, Nos 6711 and 4280.   K. Fairey

3

81A OLD OAK COMMON

Pre-Grouping Origin: GWR
Gazetteer Ref: 39 C4
Closed: 1965
Shed-Code: 81A (1949-1965)
Allocations: 1950

'County' 4-6-0
1000 *County of Middlesex*
1003 *County of Wilts*
1008 *County of Cardigan*
1010 *County of Caernarvon*
1012 *County of Denbigh*
1015 *County of Gloucester*
1021 *County of Montgomery*
1026 *County of Salop*

Class 15xx 0-6-0PT

1500	1502	1504
1501	1503	1505

Class 2251 0-6-0

2276	2282

Class 28xx 2-8-0

2826	2868	3813	3853
2835	2895	3852	

Class ROD 2-8-0
3017

Class 57xx 0-6-0PT

3648	7734	8761	8773	9707
3685	7791	8762	9658	9708
3688	8707	8763	9659	9709
3710	8750	8764	9661	9710
3754	8751	8765	9700	9725
4615	8753	8767	9701	9751
4644	8754	8768	9702	9754
4666	8756	8769	9703	9758
4698	8757	8770	9704	9784
4699	8759	8771	9705	
5764	8760	8772	9706	

'Castle' 4-6-0
4016 *The Somerset Light Infantry*
4037 *The South Wales Borderers*
4075 *Cardiff Castle*
5004 *Llanstephan Castle*
5014 *Goodrich Castle*
5027 *Farleigh Castle*
5029 *Nunney Castle*
5035 *Coity Castle*
5038 *Morlais Castle*
5039 *Rhuddlan Castle*
5040 *Stokesay Castle*
5043 *Earl of Mount Edgcumbe*
5044 *Earl of Dunraven*
5045 *Earl of Dudley*
5055 *Earl of Eldon*
5056 *Earl of Powis*
5065 *Newport Castle*
5066 *Wardour Castle*
5069 *Isambard Kingdom Brunel*
5081 *Lockheed-Hudson*
5085 *Evesham Abbey*
5087 *Tintern Abbey*
7001 *Sir James Milne*
7004 *Eastnor Castle*
7013 *Bristol Castle*
7024 *Powis Castle*
7025 *Sudeley Castle*
7030 *Cranbrook Castle*
7032 *Denbigh Castle*
7033 *Hartlebury Castle*

Class 47xx 2-8-0

4700	4701	4702	4705	4707

'Hall' 4-6-0
4900 *Saint Martin*
4923 *Evenley Hall*
4958 *Priory Hall*
4961 *Pyrland Hall*
5918 *Walton Hall*
5931 *Hatherley Hall*
5932 *Haydon Hall*
5936 *Oakley Hall*
5937 *Stanford Hall*
5938 *Stanley Hall*
5939 *Tangley Hall*
5940 *Whitbourne Hall*
5941 *Campion Hall*
5947 *Saint Benet's Hall*
5952 *Cogan Hall*
5962 *Wantage Hall*
5986 *Arbury Hall*
5987 *Brocket Hall*
5996 *Mytton Hall*
6900 *Abney Hall*
6910 *Gossington Hall*
6926 *Holkham Hall*
6932 *Burwarton Hall*
6944 *Fledborough Hall*
6953 *Leighton Hall*
6959 *Peatling Hall*
6960 *Raveningham Hall*
6962 *Soughton Hall*
6973 *Bricklehampton Hall*
6974 *Bryngwyn Hall*
6983 *Otterington Hall*
6985 *Parwick Hall*
6990 *Witherslack Hall*
7902 *Eaton Mascot Hall*
7903 *Foremarke Hall*
7904 *Fountains Hall*
7911 *Lady Margaret Hall*

'King' 4-6-0
6001 *King Edward VII*
6002 *King William IV*
6003 *King George IV*
6007 *King William III*
6009 *King Charles II*
6013 *King Henry VIII*
6014 *King Henry VII*
6015 *King Richard III*
6017 *King Edward IV*
6018 *King Henry VI*

4

6019 *King Henry V*
6021 *King Richard II*
6028 *King George VI*

Class 61xx 2-6-2T
6117	6135	6142	6155	6168
6120	6137	6144	6158	
6121	6141	6149	6159	

Class 43xx 2-6-0
| 9302 | 9305 | 9308 | 9315 |
| 9304 | 9306 | 9309 | |

Class 94xx 0-6-0PT
| 9401 | 9403 | 9405 | 9418 | 9422 |
| 9402 | 9404 | 9406 | 9419 | |

Class WD 2-8-0
| 90101 | 90105 | | *Total 193* |

Allocations: 1959

Class 15xx 0-6-0PT
| 1500 | 1503 | 1504 | 1505 |

Class 2251 0-6-0
| 2222 | 2276 | 2282 |

Class 57xx 0-6-0PT
3648	8751	8764	9659	9709
3688	8753	8765	9661	9710
3754	8754	8767	9700	9725
4615	8756	8768	9701	9751
4644	8757	8769	9702	9754
5717	8759	8770	9703	9758
5764	8760	8771	9704	9784
7722	8761	8772	9705	
7734	8762	8773	9706	
7791	8763	9658	9707	

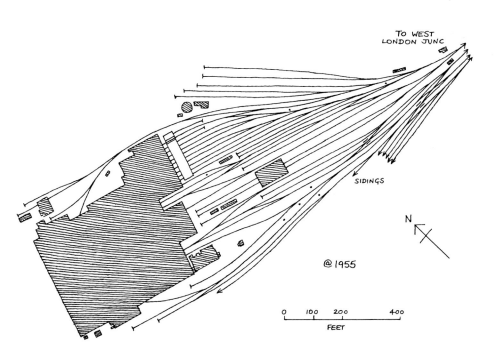

TO WEST LONDON JUNC

SIDINGS

@ 1955

N

```
0     100   200        400
|-----|-----|----------|
         FEET
```

'Castle' 4-6-0
4082 Windsor Castle
4090 Dorchester Castle
4096 Highclere Castle
5008 Raglan Castle
5014 Goodrich Castle
5027 Farleigh Castle
5034 Corfe Castle
5035 Coity Castle
5040 Stokesay Castle
5043 Earl of Mount Edgcumbe
5044 Earl of Dunraven
5052 Earl of Radnor
5056 Earl of Powis
5060 Earl of Berkeley
5065 Newport Castle
5066 Sir Felix Pole
5074 Hampden
5082 Swordfish
5084 Reading Abbey
5087 Tintern Abbey
5093 Upton Castle
7001 Sir James Milne
7004 Eastnor Castle
7008 Swansea Castle
7010 Avondale Castle
7013 Bristol Castle
7017 G. J. Churchward
7020 Gloucester Castle
7024 Powis Castle
7025 Sudeley Castle
7027 Thornbury Castle
7030 Cranbrook Castle
7032 Denbigh Castle
7033 Hartlebury Castle
7036 Taunton Castle

Class 47xx 2-8-0

| 4700 | 4701 | 4702 | 4704 | 4708 |

'Hall' 4-6-0
4900 Saint Martin
4919 Donnington Hall
5923 Colston Hall
5929 Hanham Hall
5931 Hatherley Hall
5932 Haydon Hall
5936 Oakley Hall
5939 Tangley Hall
5940 Whitbourne Hall
5941 Campion Hall
5954 Faendre Hall
5958 Knolton Hall
5976 Ashwicke Hall
5987 Brocket Hall
6920 Barningham Hall
6942 Eshton Hall
6959 Peatling Hall
6961 Stedham Hall
6962 Soughton Hall
6966 Witchingham Hall

An unidentified 'Hall' 4-6-0 alongside the coaler at Old Oak Common in 1959. Photomatic

6973 *Bricklehampton Hall*
6974 *Bryngwyn Hall*
6978 *Haroldstone Hall*
6990 *Witherslack Hall*
7902 *Eaton Mascot Hall*
7903 *Foremarke Hall*
7904 *Fountains Hall*
7927 *Willington Hall*

'King' 4-6-0
6000 *King George V*
6002 *King William IV*
6003 *King George IV*
6009 *King Charles II*
6012 *King Edward VI*
6013 *King Henry VIII*
6015 *King Richard III*
6018 *King Henry VI*
6019 *King Henry V*
6022 *King Edward III*
6023 *King Edward II*
6024 *King Edward I*
6028 *King George VI*

Class 61xx 2-6-2T

6110	6120	6135	6144	6158
6111	6121	6141	6145	6159
6113	6132	6142	6149	6168

Class 94xx 0-6-0PT

8434	9410	9414	9419	9479
8459	9411	9416	9420	
9400	9412	9418	9423	

Two 'Hall' 4-6-0s at the entrance of Old Oak's north-easterly quadrant in September 1957. Nearest the camera is No 7902 Eaton Mascot Hall *with No 6930* Aldersey Hall *beyond.* J. Peden

Class 9F 2-10-0

| 92229 | 92238 | 92240 | 92244 | 92246 |
| 92230 | 92239 | 92241 | 92245 | 92247 |

Total 173

Old Oak Common was the largest shed on the Great Western network and catered for the nearby Paddington passenger and goods termini. The assembly of its many allocated named classes within the quadrupled roundhouse was an awe inspiring sight which could never adequately be captured on film.

The covered accommodation was reduced in 1964 as demolition began to alter the site for diesel occupation. The remaining steam locos were transferred to Southall 81C in March 1965, but a few were placed in store.

7

81B SLOUGH

Pre-Grouping Origin: GWR
Gazetteer Ref: 10 G1
Closed: 1964
Shed-Code: 81B (1949-1964)
Allocations: 1950

Class 14xx 0-4-2T
1437   1442

Class 2021 0-6-0PT
2112

Class 57xx 0-6-0PT
3738	4691	5737	9653
4606	5715	5783	9781
4650	5717	9640	9789

Class 54xx 0-6-0PT
5409

Class 61xx 2-6-2T
6104	6115	6131	6150	6161
6106	6116	6133	6151	6164
6107	6119	6136	6152	
6108	6123	6140	6154	
6113	6124	6143	6157	
6114	6127	6146	6160	

Class 74xx 0-6-0PT
7441   7442

Class 94xx 0-6-0PT
| 9414 | 9415 | 9421 | 9424 |

Total 48

Allocations: 1959

Class 14xx 0-4-2T
1448   1450

Class 57xx 0-6-0PT
| 3608 | 4606 | 4650 | 5755 | 9722 |
| 3697 | 4638 | 4691 | 5766 | 9781 |

Class 61xx 2-6-2T
6108	6122	6127	6146	6154
6109	6123	6133	6150	6164
6115	6124	6136	6151	6167
6117	6126	6143	6152	

Class 94xx 0-6-0PT
| 9406 | 9415 | 9421 | 9424 | 9463 |

Total 36

The absence of any tender classes in the allocations is evidence of Slough's devotion to local duties. Of the 1950 list, the '14xx' class were used on the Windsor and Marlow branches whilst the '74xx' engines worked the Watlington line. However, the shed did host the occasional 'Jubilee' and 'Black Five' when Special trains were run to Windsor.

The depot closed in June 1964 and the remaining locos were transferred to Southall 81C.

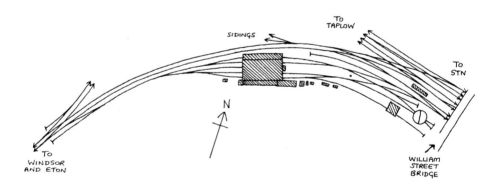

@1956

The Western end of Slough shed in September 1963. W. T. Stubbs

Slough from a north-easterly vantage point in the year of closure, 1964. J. L. Stevenson

81C SOUTHALL

Pre-Grouping Origin: GWR
Gazetteer Ref: 39 C1
Closed: 1965
Shed-Code: 81C (1949-1965)
Allocations: 1950

Class 14xx 0-4-2T
1443   1462

Class 16xx 0-6-0PT
1605

Class 1901 0-6-0PT
1925

Class 2251 0-6-0
2285

Class 28xx 2-8-0
2843	3803	3855	3857
2858	3854	3856	

Class 57xx 0-6-0PT
3618	3799	5727	7730	8774
3620	4608	5751	7731	9641
3704	4610	5753	7732	9726
3727	4673	5755	8752	
3750	4695	5799	8758	

'Hall' 4-6-0
4917 *Crosswood Hall*
4944 *Middleton Hall*
4978 *Westwood Hall*
5983 *Henley Hall*
5989 *Cransley Hall*
6961 *Stedham Hall*
7910 *Hown Hall*

Class 43xx 2-6-0
5356	6325	9300	9310
5360	6388	9301	9311

Class 54xx 0-6-0PT
5401	5410	5415	5418
5405	5414	5416	5420

Class 61xx 2-6-2T
6102	6126	6147	6165
6110	6128	6148	6169
6125	6139	6156	

@ 1961

400
200
100
0
FEET

N

To
EALING

To
STATION

An overall view of Southall yard from the west in 1963. W. T. Stubbs

Class 94xx 0-6-0PT
9407   9409

Total 71

Allocations: 1959

Class 14xx 0-4-2T
1420   1431

Class 15xx 0-6-0PT
1501

Class 57xx 0-6-0PT

3618	3750	5753	8752	9789
3620	3799	5799	8774	
3704	4608	7731	9641	
3715	4673	8750	9726	

Class 28xx 2-8-0
3836

Class 47xx 2-8-0
4707

'Hall' 4-6-0
4907 *Broughton Hall*
4925 *Eynsham Hall*
4934 *Hindlip Hall*
4996 *Eden Hall*
5918 *Walton Hall*
5925 *Eastcote Hall*
5933 *Kingsway Hall*
5996 *Mytton Hall*
6967 *Willesley Hall*
6991 *Acton Burnell Hall*
7910 *Hown Hall*
7923 *Speke Hall*

Class 54xx 0-6-0PT
5410

Class 61xx 2-6-2T

6125	6147	6156	6165
6128	6148	6157	6169

Class 94xx 0-6-0PT

8413	9405	9413	9422
8456	9409	9417	9469

Class WD 2-8-0

90152	90268	90356	90630
90174	90355	90466	

Total 58

Allocations: 1965

Class 57xx 0-6-0PT

3608	3763	4611	9659
3620	4609	4638	9726

Class 28xx 2-8-0

3812	3820	3851	3859
3818	3848	3854	3866

Class 61xx 2-6-2T

6106	6132	6141	6160	6165
6112	6134	6143	6161	6167
6117	6135	6156	6163	

'Hall' 4-6-0
6959 *Peatling Hall*
6998 *Burton Agnes Hall*
7922 *Salford Hall*

Class 94xx 0-6-0PT

8498	9418	9463	9477	9495

Class 9F 2-10-0

92216	92240	92241	92246

Total 42

In 1953/4 Southall shed was completely rebuilt from a modest single-ended 6 lane depot to a larger double-ended establishment (see diagram).

The shed closed in December 1965, but the allocation was transferred away in September of the same year. The majority of the engines went to Oxford 81F.

A Woodford Halse '8F' 2-8-0, No 48011 at the head of a line of locos at the eastern end of Southall shed in 1964. K. Fairey

81D READING

Pre-Grouping Origin: GWR
Gazetteer Ref: 4 A2
Closed: 1965
Shed-Code: 81D (1949-1965)
Allocations: 1950

Class MSWJ 2-4-0
1335   1336

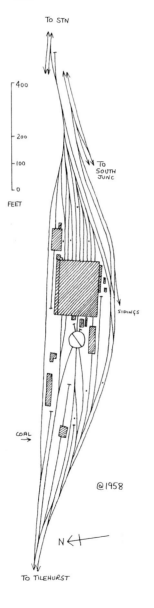

To STN

400

200

100

0

FEET

To SOUTH JUNC

SIDINGS

COAL →

@ 1958

N ←

To TILEHURST

Class 14xx 0-4-2T
1407   1444   1447

Class 2251 0-6-0
2208   2245   2264   2299

Class 2301 0-6-0
2573

Class ROD 2-8-0
3025   3047

'Bulldog' 4-4-0
3454 Skylark

Class 57xx 0-6-0PT

3697	4609	5762	7708	9749
3715	4661	5763	7777	9763
3723	4665	5766	7788	9791
3736	4670	5772	9722	

Class 28xx 2-8-0
3840   3841   3845   3846

'Castle' 4-6-0
4085 Berkeley Castle
5036 Lyonshall Castle

'Hall' 4-6-0
4920 Dumbleton Hall
4931 Hanbury Hall
4939 Littleton Hall
4943 Marrington Hall
4962 Ragley Hall
4989 Cherwell Hall
4994 Downton Hall
4995 Easton Hall
4998 Eyton Hall
5901 Hazel Hall
5933 Kingsway Hall
5948 Siddington Hall
5956 Horsley Hall
5957 Hutton Hall
5959 Mawley Hall
5973 Rolleston Hall
5979 Cruckton Hall
6968 Woodcock Hall
6996 Blackwell Hall
7919 Runter Hall

Class 43xx 2-6-0

5375	6363	6393	9307
6302	6366	7318	9313
6312	6379	7320	9318
6334	6383	9303	9319

Class 61xx 2-6-2T

6100	6103	6130	6153	6163
6101	6105	6145	6162	

'Grange' 4-6-0
6802 Bampton Grange
6864 Dymock Grange
6865 Hopton Grange

12

Class 94xx 0-6-0PT

9410	9411	9412	9420	9423

Total 91

Allocations: 1959

Class 14xx 0-4-2T

1407	1444

Class 2251 0-6-0

2212	2245	2262	2299	3219

Class 57xx 0-6-0PT

3723	4641	4670	9749
3738	4661	7708	9763
4609	4665	7788	9791

'Castle' 4-6-0
4092 *Dunraven Castle*
5010 *Restormel Castle*
5018 *St Mawes Castle*
5036 *Lyonshall Castle*
5061 *Earl of Birkenhead*

'Hall' 4-6-0
4961 *Pyrland Hall*
4962 *Ragley Hall*
4977 *Watcombe Hall*
4987 *Brockley Hall*
4989 *Cherwell Hall*
4993 *Dalton Hall*
4998 *Eyton Hall*
5901 *Hazel Hall*
5906 *Lawton Hall*
5907 *Marble Hall*
5915 *Trentham Hall*
5942 *Doldowlod Hall*

5957 *Hutton Hall*
5973 *Rolleston Hall*
5977 *Beckford Hall*
5979 *Cruckton Hall*
5982 *Harrington Hall*
5993 *Kirby Hall*
6923 *Croxteth Hall*
6924 *Grantley Hall*
6953 *Leighton Hall*
6960 *Raveningham Hall*
6968 *Woodcock Hall*
7906 *Fron Hall*
7914 *Lleweni Hall*
7919 *Runter Hall*

Class 43xx 2-6-0

5322	6302	6324
5324	6313	9309

Class 61xx 2-6-2T

6101	6104	6130	6140	6162
6102	6114	6131	6153	
6103	6129	6134	6161	

Class 56xx 0-6-2T

6627	6654	6655

Class 94xx 0-6-0PT

8430	9402	9404

Total 75

Reading shed closed in January 1965 and the remaining engines went to Didcot 81E, Southall 81C and Worcester 85A.

A line of pannier tanks at the western end of Reading (GWR) shed in 1959 with '94xx' class 0-6-0PT No 9402 at the head. Photomatic

13

81E DIDCOT

Origin: GWR (1932)
Gazetteer Ref: 10 F4
Closed: 1965
Shed-Code: 81E (1949-1965)
Allocations: 1950

Class 1854 0-6-OPT

907	1861

Class MSWJ 2-4-0

1334

Class 2251 0-6-0

2202	2222	2240	2289	3211
2221	2226	2252	3210	3212

Class 2301 0-6-0

2532	2579

Class ROD 2-8-0

3024

Class 57xx 0-6-OPT

3622	3721	5735	5752
3709	4649	5744	7710

Class 43xx 2-6-0

4318	5330	5381	6329	6359
4326	5380	5397	6340	

'Hall' 4-6-0

4935 *Ketley Hall*
5903 *Keele Hall*
5935 *Norton Hall*
6923 *Croxteth Hall*
6952 *Kimberley Hall*

Class 61xx 2-6-2T

6112	6118	6132	6134	6167

Class 90xx 4-4-0

9015

Class 94xx 0-6-OPT

9413	9417

Class WD 2-8-0

90327

Total 47

Allocations: 1959

Class 15xx 0-6-OPT

1502

Class 2251 0-6-0

2214	2240	2252	3210	3212
2221	2246	3206	3211	

Class 28xx 2-8-0

2819

Class 57xx 0-6-OPT

3622	3721	5737	5783
3653	3751	5744	7705
3709	4649	5746	7772

'Hall' 4-6-0

4915 *Condover Hall*
4939 *Littleton Hall*
4959 *Purley Hall*
4965 *Rood Ashton Hall*

4969 *Shrugborough Hall*
4994 *Downton Hall*
5943 *Elmdon Hall*
6910 *Gossington Hall*
6915 *Mursley Hall*
6952 *Kimberley Hall*
6969 *Wraysbury Hall*
6983 *Otterington Hall*
6996 *Blackwell Hall*

Class 43xx 2-6-0

| 5326 | 6379 | 7324 |
| 5380 | 6388 | 7327 |

Class 56xx 0-6-2T

| 5639 | 5647 | 5697 |

Class 94xx 0-6-0PT

| 8435 | 8458 | 9407 |

Total 48

Allocations: 1965

'Hall' 4-6-0
4962 *Ragley Hall*
6910 *Gossington Hall*
6921 *Borwick Hall*
6928 *Underley Hall*
6937 *Conyngham Hall*
6953 *Leighton Hall*
6961 *Stedham Hall*
6963 *Throwley Hall*
6983 *Otterington Hall*
6991 *Acton Burnell Hall*
7917 *North Aston Hall*

Class 61xx 2-6-2T

| 6136 | 6145 | 6159 |

'Manor' 4-6-0
7814 *Fringford Manor*
7816 *Frilsham Manor*
7829 *Ramsbury Manor*

Class 57xx 0-6-0PT
8720

Total 18

Didcot closed in June 1965 and the remaining stock went to Oxford 81F and Gloucester Horton Road 85B.
The shed still exists and houses much of the Great Western Society's privately preserved rolling stock.

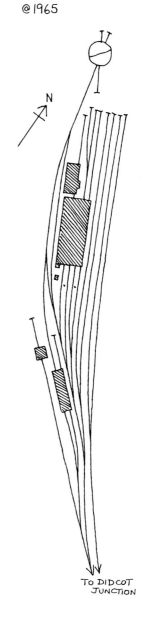

@ 1965

To DIDCOT
JUNCTION

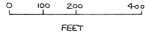

| 0 | 100 | 200 | 400 |

FEET

A view of Didcot MPD in July 1964.   J. L. Stevenson

15

81F OXFORD

Pre-Grouping Origin: GWR
Gazetteer Ref: 10 E4
Closed: 1966
Shed-Code: 81F (1949-1966)
Allocations: 1950

Class 14xx 0-4-2T
| 1448 | 1450 |

Class 16xx 0-6-0PT
1617

Class 1901 0-6-0PT
1935

Class 2021 0-6-0PT
2076

Class 2251 0-6-0
2249

Class 28xx 2-8-0
| 2827 | 2860 | 3847 |
| 2845 | 3835 | 3866 |

Class 57xx 0-6-0PT
| 3608 | 4645 | 4680 | 9611 |
| 3722 | 4676 | 7760 | 9654 |

'Star' 4-6-0
4021 British Monarch

Class 45xx 2-6-2T
| 4511 | 4513 | 4558 |

'Hall' 4-6-0
4902 Aldenham Hall
4903 Astley Hall
4921 Eaton Hall
4928 Gatacre Hall
4938 Liddington Hall
5904 Kelham Hall
5960 Saint Edmund Hall
5965 Woollas Hall
6925 Hackness Hall
6933 Birtles Hall
6937 Conyngham Hall
6970 Whaddon Hall

Class 43xx 2-6-0
| 5323 | 6300 | 6313 | 9316 | 9317 |

Class 54xx 0-6-0PT
5413

Class 61xx 2-6-2T
| 6109 | 6111 | 6122 | 6138 |

'Castle' 4-6-0
7008 Swansea Castle
7010 Avondale Castle

Class 74xx 0-6-0PT
| 7404 | 7411 | 7412 | 7436 |

Class 94xx 0-6-0PT
9416

Class WD 2-8-0
90529

Total 54

Allocations: 1959

Class 14xx 0-4-2T
| 1435 | 1442 | 1447 | 5818 |

Class 28xx 2-8-0
| 2836 | 2880 | 3814 | 3823 | 3857 |

Class 57xx 0-6-0PT
| 3722 | 9611 | 9653 |
| 7760 | 9640 | 9654 |

Class 51xx 2-6-2T
| 4125 | 4147 | 4148 | 5190 |

'Hall' 4-6-0
4902 Aldenham Hall
4903 Astley Hall
4921 Eaton Hall
4938 Liddington Hall
4954 Plaish Hall
4979 Wootton Hall
4995 Easton Hall
5960 Saint Edmund Hall
5966 Ashford Hall
6922 Burton Hall
6927 Lilford Hall
6937 Conyngham Hall
6970 Whaddon Hall
7900 Saint Peter's Hall
7911 Lady Margaret Hall

'Castle' 4-6-0
5012 Berry Pomeroy Castle
5025 Chirk Castle
5033 Broughton Castle

Class 61xx 2-6-2T
| 6106 | 6112 | 6138 | 6163 |

Class 56xx 0-6-2T
6664

'Grange' 4-6-0
6821 Leaton Grange
6822 Manton Grange
6848 Toddington Grange
6854 Roundhill Grange
6858 Woolston Grange
6864 Dymock Grange

Class 72xx 2-8-2T
| 7238 | 7239 |

Class 74xx 0-6-0PT
| 7404 | 7411 | 7412 |

Class 94xx 0-6-0PT
| 8424 | 8432 | 9403 | 9450 |

16

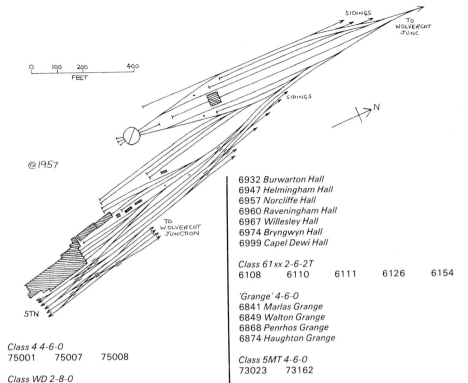

@1957

STN

```
0    100   200        400
|    |     |          |
        FEET
```

N

Class 4 4-6-0
75001   75007   75008

Class WD 2-8-0
90251   90284

Total 62

Allocations: 1965

Class 57xx 0-6-0PT
3751   9653   9773   9789

'Hall' 4-6-0
5933 *Kingsway Hall*
6923 *Croxteth Hall*
6924 *Grantley Hall*
6927 *Lilford Hall*

6932 *Burwarton Hall*
6947 *Helmingham Hall*
6957 *Norcliffe Hall*
6960 *Raveningham Hall*
6967 *Willesley Hall*
6974 *Bryngwyn Hall*
6999 *Capel Dewi Hall*

Class 61xx 2-6-2T
6108   6110   6111   6126   6154

'Grange' 4-6-0
6841 *Marlas Grange*
6849 *Walton Grange*
6868 *Penrhos Grange*
6874 *Haughton Grange*

Class 5MT 4-6-0
73023   73162

Total 26

Oxford shed closed in January 1966 and was the last ex-GWR depot with steam power on the Western Region. Many other ex-GWR sheds survived after this date (eg Tyseley and Weymouth) but only as constitutents of other regions.
    Oxford's last locos all went for scrap.

Further evidence for Oxford shed's cosmopolitan atmosphere. A 'West Country' 4-6-2 No 34022 Exmoor *(70D Eastleigh) at the depot in 1964 alongside 'Grange' 4-6-0 No 6874* Haughton Grange. *K. Fairey*

82A BRISTOL BATH ROAD

Origin: GWR (1934)
Gazetteer Ref: 3 G1
Closed: 1960
Shed-Code: 82A (1949-1960)
Allocations: 1950

'County' 4-6-0
1002 *County of Berks*
1005 *County of Devon*
1007 *County of Brecknock*
1011 *County of Chester*
1014 *County of Glamorgan*
1028 *County of Warwick*

Class 14xx 0-4-2T
1415   1430   1463   5809   5813

Class 2021 0-6-0PT
2072

Class 2301 0-6-0
2445   2534

'Saint' 4-6-0
2931 *Arlington Court*
2939 *Croome Court*
2948 *Stackpole Court*
2950 *Taplow Court*

'Star' 4-6-0
4020 *Knight Commander*
4033 *Queen Victoria*
4034 *Queen Adelaide*
4035 *Queen Charlotte*
4041 *Prince of Wales*
4042 *Prince Albert*
4043 *Prince Henry*
4047 *Princess Louise*
4056 *Princess Margaret*

'Castle' 4-6-0
4073 *Caerphilly Castle*
4084 *Aberystwyth Castle*
4091 *Dudley Castle*
4093 *Dunster Castle*
4096 *Highclere Castle*
5000 *Launceston Castle*
5018 *St Mawes Castle*
5019 *Treago Castle*
5025 *Chirk Castle*
5037 *Monmouth Castle*
5048 *Earl of Devon*
5067 *St Fagans Castle*
5074 *Hampden*
5076 *Gladiator*
5082 *Swordfish*
5094 *Tretower Castle*
5096 *Bridgwater Castle*
7011 *Banbury Castle*
7014 *Caerhays Castle*
7019 *Fowey Castle*

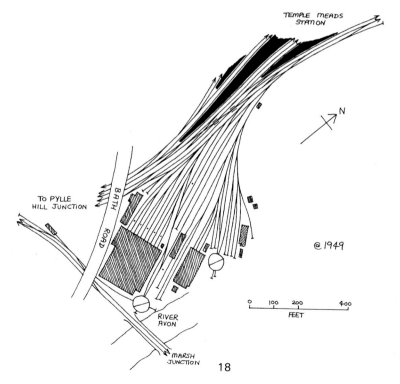

18

Looking south to Bristol Bath Road shed from the platforms of Temple Meads station in 1955.
N. E. Preedy

7034 *Ince Castle*

Class 51xx 2-6-2T
4142	4151	4155
4143	4152	5169

Class 45xx 2-6-2T
4535	4595	5527	5547	5561
4536	5506	5528	5548	5564
4539	5511	5535	5553	5572
4563	5512	5536	5555	
4577	5514	5539	5558	
4580	5523	5546	5559	

'Hall' 4-6-0
4914 *Cranmore Hall*
4942 *Maindy Hall*
4951 *Pendeford Hall*
4954 *Plaish Hall*
4985 *Allesley Hall*
6954 *Lotherton Hall*
6958 *Oxburgh Hall*
6965 *Thirlestaine Hall*
6972 *Beningbrough Hall*
6977 *Grundisburgh Hall*
6981 *Marbury Hall*
6997 *Bryn-Ivor Hall*

7901 *Dodington Hall*
7917 *North Aston Hall*

Class 43xx 2-6-0
5311	5325	5327	6351

'King' 4-6-0
6000 *King George V*

Total 100

Allocations: 1959
'County' 4-6-0
1000 *County of Middlesex*
1005 *County of Devon*
1009 *County of Carmarthen*
1011 *County of Chester*
1014 *County of Glamorgan*
1024 *County of Pembroke*
1028 *County of Warwick*

Class 14xx 0-4-2T
1409	1412	1454	1463

Class 57xx 0-6-0PT
3677	3748	4619	9623	9729
3720	3759	8741	9626	9771

'Castle' 4-6-0
4075 *Cardiff Castle*
4078 *Pembroke Castle*
4079 *Pendennis Castle*
4080 *Powderham Castle*
4081 *Warwick Castle*
5015 *Kingswear Castle*
5048 *Earl of Devon*

19

Another view of Bath Road from the station, this time in 1953. Real Photos

5054 *Earl of Ducie*
5057 *Earl Waldegrave*
5062 *Earl of Shaftesbury*
5073 *Blenheim*
5076 *Gladiator*
5078 *Beaufort*
5085 *Evesham Abbey*
5090 *Neath Abbey*
5092 *Tresco Abbey*
5096 *Bridgwater Castle*
7003 *Elmley Castle*
7011 *Banbury Castle*
7014 *Caerhays Castle*
7015 *Carn Brea Castle*
7018 *Drysllwyn Castle*
7019 *Fowey Castle*
7034 *Ince Castle*

Class 51xx 2-6-2T
4163   5186   5197

'Hall' 4-6-0
4922 *Enville Hall*
4927 *Farnborough Hall*
4947 *Nanhoran Hall*
4988 *Bulwell Hall*
5949 *Trematon Hall*
5950 *Wardley Hall*
6900 *Abney Hall*
6908 *Downham Hall*

6919 *Tylney Hall*
6954 *Lotherton Hall*
6957 *Norcliffe Hall*
6972 *Beningbrough Hall*
6981 *Marbury Hall*
6982 *Melmerby Hall*
6997 *Bryn-Ivor Hall*
7901 *Dodington Hall*
7907 *Hart Hall*

Class 43xx 2-6-0
5311   6363

Class 45xx 2-6-2T
5529   5530   5536   5561

Class 61xx 2-6-2T
6107

Class 94xx 0-6-0PT
9481   9488

Class 2 2-6-2T
41202   41203   41249

Class 3 2-6-2T
82007   82035   82042   82044
82033   82040   82043

Total 84

Bristol Bath Road was closed in September 1960 and the remaining locos went to neighbouring sheds at Bristol St Philips Marsh 82B and Barrow Road 92E (ex-LMR 22A).

82B ST PHILIPS MARSH

Pre-Grouping Origin: GWR
Gazetteer Ref: 3 G1
Closed: 1964
Shed-Code: 82B (1949-1964)
Allocations: 1950

Class 2021 0-6-0PT
2031   2070   2135

Class 2251 0-6-0
2215   2225   2253   2269   3215
2220   2251   2265   2293

Class 2301 0-6-0
2322   2340   2462   2578

Class 28xx 2-8-0
2818   2844   2859
2839   2846   3842

Class ROD 2-8-0
3014   3032   3034   3041

Class 57xx 0-6-0PT
3604   3765   5784   7790   8747
3614   3773   7711   7793   8766
3623   3784   7718   7795   8790
3632   3795   7719   8702   8795
3643   4603   7726   8703   9604
3676   4607   7728   8713   9605
3720   4619   7729   8714   9606
3731   4624   7749   8722   9620
3746   4626   7779   8730   9626
3759   4655   7780   8737   9665
3763   4660   7782   8741   9729
3764   4688   7783   8746   9764

Class 42xx 2-8-0T
4262

Class 47xx 2-8-0
4706

'Hall' 4-6-0
4907 *Broughton Hall*
4909 *Blakesley Hall*
4916 *Crumlin Hall*
4934 *Hindlip Hall*
4948 *Northwick Hall*
4967 *Shirenewton Hall*
4969 *Shrugborough Hall*
4986 *Aston Hall*
4990 *Clifton Hall*
4999 *Gopsal Hall*
5919 *Worsley Hall*
5949 *Trematon Hall*
5982 *Harrington Hall*
5992 *Horton Hall*
6909 *Frewin Hall*
6914 *Langton Hall*
6922 *Burton Hall*
6957 *Norcliffe Hall*
6986 *Rydal Hall*

7900 *Saint Peter's Hall*
7906 *Fron Hall*
7907 *Hart Hall*
7908 *Henshall Hall*

Class 43xx 2-6-0
5351   5358

Class 56xx 0-6-2T
6601   6656   6670   6671

'Grange' 4-6-0
6805 *Broughton Grange*
6811 *Cranbourne Grange*
6827 *Llanfrechfa Grange*
6830 *Buckenhill Grange*
6832 *Brockton Grange*
6836 *Estevarney Grange*
6837 *Forthampton Grange*
6840 *Hazeley Grange*
6842 *Nunhold Grange*
6846 *Ruckley Grange*
6849 *Walton Grange*
6850 *Cleeve Grange*
6852 *Headbourne Grange*
6861 *Crynant Grange*
6863 *Dolhywel Grange*
6867 *Peterston Grange*
6876 *Kingsland Grange*

Class 81xx 2-6-2T
8105

Class 94xx 0-6-0PT
8413

Class WD 2-8-0
90176   90207   90238   90356   90573

Total 141

Allocations: 1959

Class 2251 0-6-0
2205   2250   2265   3215
2213   2261   2277

Class 57xx 0-6-0PT
3604   3731   3795   7728   8747
3623   3758   4603   7729   8790

A westerly view of Bristol St Philips Marsh yard in August 1958 with '43xx' 2-6-0 No 6356 at the coaler. M. Hale

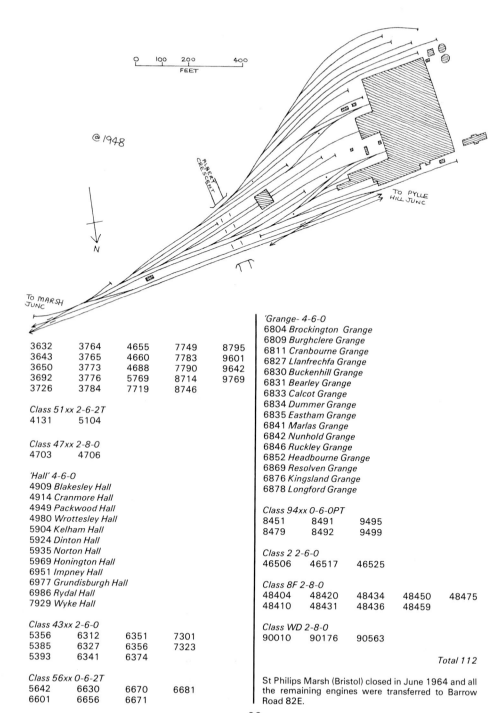

@ 1948

TO MARSH JUNC

RUPERT CRESCENT

TO PYLLE HILL JUNC

3632	3764	4655	7749	8795
3643	3765	4660	7783	9601
3650	3773	4688	7790	9642
3692	3776	5769	8714	9769
3726	3784	7719	8746	

Class 51xx 2-6-2T
4131   5104

Class 47xx 2-8-0
4703   4706

'Hall' 4-6-0
4909 *Blakesley Hall*
4914 *Cranmore Hall*
4949 *Packwood Hall*
4980 *Wrottesley Hall*
5904 *Kelham Hall*
5924 *Dinton Hall*
5935 *Norton Hall*
5969 *Honington Hall*
6951 *Impney Hall*
6977 *Grundisburgh Hall*
6986 *Rydal Hall*
7929 *Wyke Hall*

Class 43xx 2-6-0

5356	6312	6351	7301
5385	6327	6356	7323
5393	6341	6374	

Class 56xx 0-6-2T

5642	6630	6670	6681
6601	6656	6671	

'Grange- 4-6-0
6804 *Brockington Grange*
6809 *Burghclere Grange*
6811 *Cranbourne Grange*
6827 *Llanfrechfa Grange*
6830 *Buckenhill Grange*
6831 *Bearley Grange*
6833 *Calcot Grange*
6834 *Dummer Grange*
6835 *Eastham Grange*
6841 *Marlas Grange*
6842 *Nunhold Grange*
6846 *Ruckley Grange*
6852 *Headbourne Grange*
6869 *Resolven Grange*
6876 *Kingsland Grange*
6878 *Longford Grange*

Class 94xx 0-6-0PT

8451	8491	9495
8479	8492	9499

Class 2 2-6-0

46506	46517	46525

Class 8F 2-8-0

48404	48420	48434	48450	48475
48410	48431	48436	48459	

Class WD 2-8-0

90010	90176	90563

Total 112

St Philips Marsh (Bristol) closed in June 1964 and all the remaining engines were transferred to Barrow Road 82E.

82C SWINDON

Pre-Grouping Origin: GWR
Gazetteer Ref: 9 G5
Closed: 1964
Shed-Code: 82C (1949-1964)
Allocations: 1950

Class WCP 0-6-0T
5 *Portishead*

Class 1901 0-6-0PT

992	2014	2017

Class 1366 0-6-0PT

1366	1369	1371

Class 14xx 0-4-2T

1400	1433	1446	5802	5805
1403	1436	5800	5804	

Class 1501 0-6-0PT
1542

Class 2021 0-6-0PT
2060

Class BPGV 0-6-0ST
2195

Class 2251 0-6-0

2224	2250

Class 2301 0-6-0
2568

'Saint' 4-6-0
2908 *Lady of Quality*
2927 *Saint Patrick*
2934 *Butleigh Court*
2945 *Hillingdon Court*
2947 *Madresfield Court*
2949 *Stanford Court*
2954 *Tockenham Court*

'Bulldog' 4-4-0
3444 *Cormorant*
3449 *Nightingale*
3451 *Pelican*
3453 *Seagull*

Class 57xx 0-6-0PT

3645	3739	6716	8733	9772
3666	3748	6737	8779	9773
3682	3780	6739	8793	9790
3684	4612	6741	9600	9795
3724	4651	7792	9720	
3737	4697	7794	9721	

'Star' 4-6-0
4015 *Knight of St John*
4022
4036 *Queen Elizabeth*
4055 *Princess Sophia*
4057 *Princess Elizabeth*
4062 *Malmesbury Abbey*

'Castle' 4-6-0
4081 *Warwick Castle*
5009 *Shrewsbury Castle*
5068 *Beverston Castle*
5083 *Bath Abbey*
5084 *Reading Abbey*
5091 *Cleeve Abbey*
7015 *Carn Brea Castle*

Class 43xx 2-6-0

4381	5371	6322	6360	6387
5322	5396	6357	6374	7321
5367	6320	6358	6384	

Class 45xx 2-6-2T

4502	4544	4585	5510	5566
4521	4550	4590	5534	
4538	4551	4592	5563	

'Hall' 4-6-0
4925 *Eynsham Hall*
4945 *Milligan Hall*
4956 *Plowden Hall*
4973 *Sweeney Hall*
4983 *Albert Hall*
5922 *Caxton Hall*
5934 *Kneller Hall*
5943 *Elmdon Hall*
6908 *Downham Hall*
6915 *Mursley Hall*
7914 *Lleweni Hall*
7916 *Mobberley Hall*

Class 74xx 0-6-0PT

7415	7418	7424

Class 90xx 4-4-0

9011	9018	9023

'Duke' 4-4-0
9083 *Comet*
9089

Class 94xx 0-6-0PT
9400

Class WD 2-8-0

90312	90324	90589

Total 125

Allocations: 1959

'County' 4-6-0
1004 *County of Somerset*
1012 *County of Denbigh*
1019 *County of Merioneth*

Class 1361 0-6-0ST
1365

Class 1366 0-6-0PT

1369	1371

Class 14xx 0-4-2T

1410	1438	5804
1433	1464	5815

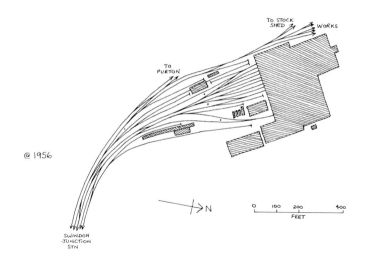

To STOCK SHED · WORKS · To PURTON · @ 1956 · →N · 0 100 200 400 FEET · SWINDON JUNCTION STN

Class 16xx 0-6-0PT				
1658				
Class 2251 0-6-0				
2203	2293			
Class 28xx 2-8-0				
2818	2835	2852	2865	2879

'City' 4-4-0
3440 *City of Truro*

Class 57xx 0-6-0PT				
3645	3739	4697	8783	9720
3666	3746	6741	8793	9721
3682	3763	6758	9600	9740
3684	3780	6769	9604	9773
3711	4612	7794	9605	9790
3724	4651	8779	9672	9795

'Castle' 4-6-0
4086 *Builth Castle*
5000 *Launceston Castle*
5002 *Ludlow Castle*
5005 *Manorbier Castle*
5007 *Rougemont Castle*
5009 *Shrewsbury Castle*
5023 *Brecon Castle*
5064 *Bishop's Castle*
5068 *Beverston Castle*
7037 *Swindon*

Class 51xx 2-6-2T
4102   4129

'Hall' 4-6-0
4953 *Pitchford Hall*
4972 *Saint Brides Hall*
5922 *Caxton Hall*
5964 *Wolseley Hall*
5978 *Bodinnick Hall*
5981 *Frensham Hall*
5983 *Henley Hall*
5986 *Arbury Hall*
5997 *Sparkford Hall*
6902 *Butlers Hall*
6993 *Arthog Hall*

Class 43xx 2-6-0				
5306	6307	6334	6366	9315
5351	6309	6336	6391	

Class 45xx 2-6-2T		
5509	5528	5540
5510	5532	5547

Class 56xx 0-6-2T
6639

Class 74xx 0-6-0PT				
7413	7418	7421	7424	7427

Class 94xx 0-6-0PT				
8433	8461	8465	8472	9476

Class 5 4-6-0		
73001	73012	73027

Class 4 4-6-0				
75000	75002	75024	75027	75029

Total 108

Swindon shed closed in November 1964 and the majority of remaining engines transferred to Didcot 81E and Gloucester Horton Road 85B.

The depot boasted the last 'County' class 4-6-0 namely No 1011 *County of Chester*, being withdrawn in the month of closure.

It will be seen that No 3440 *City of Truro*, the preserved 4-4-0, was housed at Swindon in the late 1950s, being on loan to the WR for use on special trains.

24

A variety of classes on display outside Swindon in 1954. N. E. Preedy

The interior of Swindon a month before closure, in October 1964. Left to right are Nos 7918 Rhose Wood Hall *(2A), 92232 (88A), 43940 (2E), 6850* Cleeve Grange *(86E) and 7014* Caerhays Castle *(2A).* N. E. Preedy

82D WESTBURY

Pre-Grouping Origin: GWR
Gazetteer Ref: 3 B4
Closed: 1965
Shed-Codes: 82D (1949-1963)
83C (1963-1965)
Allocations: 1950 (82D)

'County' 4-6-0
1027 County of Stafford

Class 2021 0-6-0PT
2023	2053

Class 2301 0-6-0
2426	2444

Class 57xx 0-6-0PT
3696	4647	5781	8744	9762
3735	5718	5785	9612	
3758	5757	7727	9615	
4636	5771	7784	9628	

'Star' 4-6-0
4028
4038 Queen Berengaria
4045 Prince John

Class 43xx 2-6-0
4377	5385	6368	6399	7309
5306	6314	6369	7300	
5326	6365	6375	7302	

Class 45xx 2-6-2T
4508	4572	5508	5554
4510	4573	5509	

'Hall' 4-6-0
4926 Fairleigh Hall
4927 Farnborough Hall
4963 Rignall Hall
5900 Hinderton Hall
5924 Dinton Hall
5925 Eastcote Hall
5961 Toynbee Hall
5971 Merevale Hall
5974 Wallsworth Hall
5985 Mostyn Hall
6935 Browsholme Hall
6955 Lydcott Hall
6966 Witchingham Hall
6978 Haroldstone Hall
6982 Melmerby Hall
6991 Acton Burnell Hall

Class 54xx 0-6-0PT
5402	5406	5422
5403	5419	5423

Class 56xx 0-6-2T
5689	6690	6699

'Grange' 4-6-0
6804 Brockington Grange
6845 Paviland Grange

Class WD 2-8-0
90343	90630	90701

Total 75

Allocations: 1959 (82D)

Class 2251 0-6-0
2268

Class 28xx 2-8-0
2811	3819

Class 57xx 0-6-0PT
3614	4607	5771	8744	9668
3629	4636	7727	9612	9762
3696	4647	7748	9615	
3735	5757	7784	9628	

Class 45xx 2-6-2T
4536	4567	5526	5554
4555	5508	5542	

'Hall' 4-6-0
4917 Crosswood Hall
4933 Himley Hall
4945 Milligan Hall
5945 Leckhampton Hall
5963 Wimpole Hall
5974 Wallsworth Hall
5975 Winslow Hall
6945 Glasfryn Hall
6955 Lydcott Hall
6994 Baggrave Hall
7909 Heveningham Hall
7917 North Aston Hall
7924 Thornycroft Hall

Class 43xx 2-6-0
5358	6320	6358	7300	7302

Class 54xx 0-6-0PT
5414	5416	5423

Class 56xx 0-6-2T
5689	6625

Class 64xx 0-6-0PT
6408

Class 94xx 0-6-0PT
8482

Total 53

Allocations: 1965 (83C)

Class 57xx 0-6-0PT
3669	4607	4673	9605
3735	4636	4697	9790

Total 8

Westbury closed in September 1965 and the six remaining locos were withdrawn.

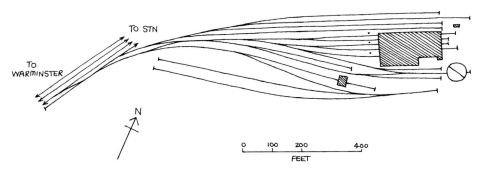

@1957

TO STN

TO WARMINSTER

N

```
0    100   200        400
          FEET
```

Westbury shed in 1949 looking east.
Real Photos

A panoramic view of Westbury shed and yard about 1960. IAL

82E YEOVIL PEN MILL

Pre-Grouping Origin: GWR
Gazetteer Ref: 3 D2
Closed: 1959
Shed-Codes: 82E (1949-1958)
71H (1958-1959)
Allocations: 1950 (82E)

Class 57xx 0-6-0PT

3671	4689	8745	9732
3733	5767	9601	9771

Class 45xx 2-6-2T

5529	5565

Total 10

Yeovil Pen Mill became Southern Region property in February 1958 and took up the code 71H.

The shed closed in January 1959 and the entire allocation was moved to Yeovil Town 72C.

Class 57xx 0-6-0PT No 9764 (82F) and Pen Mill shed in 1952.   Real Photos

A head-on view of Yeovil Pen Mill shed in July 1954, with '57xx' 0-6-0PT No 9732 of the depot keeping guard.   W. Potter

28

82F WEYMOUTH

Pre-Grouping Origin: GWR
Gazetteer Ref: 3 G3
Closed: 1967
Shed-Codes: 82F (1949-1958)
71G (1958-1963)
70G (1963-1967)
Allocations: 1950 (82F)

Class 1366 0-6-0PT
1367   1368   1370

Class 14xx 0-4-2T
1453   1454   1467

Class 1501 0-6-0PT
1789

'Saint' 4-6-0
2912 *Saint Ambrose*

'Castle' 4-6-0
4080 *Powderham Castle*

Class 45xx 2-6-2T
4507   4520   4527   4562

'Hall' 4-6-0
4930 *Hagley Hall*
4988 *Bulwell Hall*
5968 *Cory Hall*
5978 *Bodinnick Hall*
6902 *Butlers Hall*
6912 *Helmster Hall*
6945 *Glasfryn Hall*
6988 *Swithland Hall*
6993 *Arthog Hall*

Class 43xx 2-6-0
5305   5328   5338   5384
5314   5337   5359

Class 74xx 0-6-0PT
7408

Class 57xx 0-6-0PT
9642

Total 31

Allocations: 1959 (71G)

Class 1366 0-6-0PT
1367   1368   1370

Class 14xx 0-4-2T
1453   1474

Class 57xx 0-6-0PT
3737   4689   7780   8799
4624   5784   7782   9620

Class 51xx 2-6-2T
4133   4166

Class 45xx 2-6-2T
4507   4562

Class 43xx 2-6-0
5384   6344   7303

'Hall' 4-6-0
6914 *Langton Hall*

Class 5 4-6-0
73017   73018   73020   73022   73029

Total 26

@1957

To STN

TO UPWEY
JUNCTION

N

0	100	200	400

FEET

Allocations: 1965 (70G)

'Merchant Navy' 4-6-2
35005 *Canadian Pacific*
35007 *Aberdeen Commonwealth*
35012 *United States Lines*
35014 *Nederland Line*
35016 *Elders Fyffes*
35017 *Belgian Marine*
35019 *French Line CGT*
35022 *Holland-America Line*
35026 *Lamport & Holt Line*
35028 *Clan Line*
35029 *Ellerman Lines*
35030 *Elder Dempster Lines*

Class 2MT 2-6-2T
41261   41284   41298   41305   41324

Class 5MT 4-6-0
73002
73018
73020
73042
73080 *Merlin*
73083 *Pendragon*

Total 23

As the shed-codes infer, Weymouth became part of the Southern Region from February 1958, using the code 71G. In September 1963 the code was altered to 70G.

Closing in July 1967, the shed enjoyed two distinctions as the last ex-GWR shed with steam (albeit with SR stock) and one of the last seven steam sheds on the Southern Region. All the remaining locos went for scrap.

Looking north to Weymouth shed in 1950.
LGRP, courtesy David & Charles

Weymouth shed and sidings as viewed from the buffer stops in 1962 when in Southern Region control as 71G. Excursion traffic is well in evidence and the three locos nearest the camera are, (left to right) 'West Country' 4-6-2 No 34042 Dorchester (71B), 'Battle of Britain' 4-6-2 No 34066 Spitfire (72A) and Class 4 2-6-0 No 76025 (71B)
D. H. Cape

83A NEWTON ABBOT

Pre-Grouping Origin: GWR
Gazetteer Ref: 2 C3
Closed: 1963
Shed-Code: 83A (1949-1963)
Allocations: 1950

'County' 4-6-0
1018 County of Leicester
1019 County of Merioneth

Class 1361 0-6-0ST
1362

Class 14xx 0-4-2T
1427   1439   1466   1470

Class 16xx 0-6-0PT
1608

Class 2181 0-6-0PT
2181   2183

Class 28xx 2-8-0
2809   2881

Class 57xx 0-6-0PT
3600   5798   9633   9778
3659   9623   9668

'Castle' 4-6-0
4077 Chepstow Castle
4098 Kidwelly Castle
4099 Kilgerran Castle
5011 Tintagel Castle
5024 Carew Castle
5028 Llantilio Castle
5034 Corfe Castle
5041 Tiverton Castle

5047 Earl of Dartmouth
5071 Spitfire
5078 Beaufort
5079 Lysander
7000 Viscount Portal
7029 Clun Castle

Class 51xx 2-6-2T
4109   5108   5140   5153
4133   5113   5142   5157
4179   5132   5150   5158

Class 44xx 2-6-2T
4405

Class 45xx 2-6-2T
4532   4582   5505   5551   5557
4547   4587   5544   5552

'Hall' 4-6-0
4950 Patshull Hall
5920 Wycliffe Hall
6934 Beachamwell Hall

Class 43xx 2-6-0
5350   5391   6345

'Grange' 4-6-0
6813 Eastbury Grange
6814 Enbourne Grange
6822 Manton Grange
6829 Burmington Grange

Looking north to the running shed at Newton Abbot in September 1959.   D. S. Fish

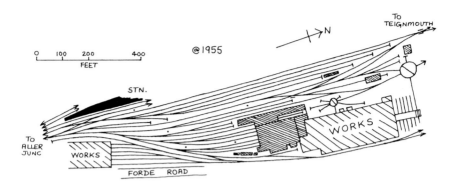

@1955

FEET
0   100   200   400

STN.

To ALLER JUNC

WORKS

WORKS

FORDE ROAD

To TEIGNMOUTH

N

Class 72xx 2-8-2T
7200	7209	7220	7250

Class 74xx 0-6-0PT
7427

'Manor' 4-6-0
7812 *Erlestoke Manor*
7813 *Freshford Manor*

Class 94xx 0-6-0PT
8403

Total 73

Allocations: 1959

Class 14xx 0-4-2T
1452	1466	1470

Class 16xx 0-6-0PT
1608

Class 28xx 2-8-0
2805	2846	2881	3840	3864
2807	2875	3834	3841	

Class 57xx 0-6-0PT
3659	3796	9633	9678

'Castle' 4-6-0
4037 *The South Wales Borderers*
4083 *Abbotsbury Castle*
4084 *Aberystwyth Castle*
4098 *Kidwelly Castle*
5003 *Lulworth Castle*
5011 *Tintagel Castle*
5024 *Carew Castle*
5032 *Usk Castle*
5049 *Earl of Plymouth*
5053 *Earl Cairns*
5055 *Earl of Eldon*
5079 *Lysander*
7000 *Viscount Portal*
7029 *Clun Castle*

Class 51xx 2-6-2T
4105	4174	4179	5158	5195
4108	4176	5150	5164	5196
4145	4177	5153	5178	
4150	4178	5154	5183	

Class 45xx 2-6-2T
4561	5558	5573

'Hall' 4-6-0
4905 *Barton Hall*
4920 *Dumbleton Hall*
4936 *Kinlet Hall*
4955 *Plaspower Hall*
4967 *Shirenewton Hall*
4975 *Umberslade Hall*
5920 *Wycliffe Hall*
5967 *Bickmarsh Hall*
6933 *Birtles Hall*
6938 *Carndean Hall*
6940 *Didlington Hall*
7916 *Mobberley Hall*

Class 43xx 2-6-0
6360

Class 56xx 0-6-2T
6614

'Grange' 4-6-0
6813 *Eastbury Grange*
6829 *Burmington Grange*
6836 *Estevarney Grange*
6859 *Yiewsley Grange*

Class 74xx 0-6-0PT
7445

Class 94xx 0-6-0PT
9440	9462	9487

Total 74

Newton Abbot was responsible for loco overhauls for the south-west area and possessed a large works for the purpose (see map).

The bulk of the allocation was transferred away in mid-1962 but final closure came in January 1963 when the last few remaining locos went to Carmarthen 87G and Llanelly 87F.

83B TAUNTON

Pre-Grouping Origin: GWR
Gazetteer Ref: 8 F4
Closed: 1964
Shed-Code: 83B (1949-1964)
Allocations: 1950

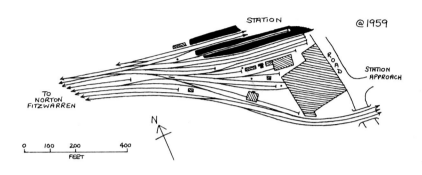

Cardiff Railway 0-4-0ST
1338

Class 2021 0-6-0PT
2038   2127

Class BPGV 0-6-0ST
2194 *Kidwelly*

Class 2251 0-6-0
| 2211 | 2213 | 2261 | 2267 | 2275 |
| 2212 | 2214 | 2266 | 2268 | |

Class 28xx 2-8-0
2814

Class 57xx 0-6-0PT
| 3669 | 4663 | 9663 | 9718 |
| 4604 | 9646 | 9670 | 9757 |

Class 51xx 2-6-2T
| 4113 | 4117 | 4136 | 5172 |

'Hall' 4-6-0
4949 *Packwood Hall*
4970 *Sketty Hall*
4971 *Stanway Hall*
5999 *Wollaton Hall*
6995 *Benthall Hall*

'Castle' 4-6-0
5003 *Lulworth Castle*
5077 *Fairey Castle*

Class 54xx 0-6-0PT
5412

Class 45xx 2-6-2T
| 5501 | 5504 | 5522 | 5542 | 5571 |
| 5503 | 5521 | 5533 | 5543 | |

Class 43xx 2-6-0
6305	6328	6372	6398
6317	6343	6377	7304
6323	6364	6394	

'Grange' 4-6-0
6815 *Frilford Grange*
6868 *Penrhos Grange*
6875 *Hindford Grange*

Class 74xx 0-6-0PT
7421

Total 58

Allocations: 1959

Cardiff Railway 0-4-0ST
1338

Class 1361 0-6-0ST
1362

Class 1366 0-6-0PT
1366

Class 16xx 0-6-0PT
1668

33

Class 2251 0-6-0
2235

Class 28xx 2-8-0
2822

Class 57xx 0-6-0PT

3669	5721	9608	9670
3736	5779	9646	9671
4604	5780	9647	9718
4663	5798	9663	9757

Class 51xx 2-6-2T

4128	4157	4159	5185

'Hall' 4-6-0
4930 Hagley Hall
4932 Hatherton Hall
4940 Ludford Hall
4970 Sketty Hall
4971 Stanway Hall
4978 Westwood Hall
4985 Allesley Hall
4991 Cobham Hall
5992 Horton Hall
5999 Wollaton Hall
6995 Benthall Hall

Class 45xx 2-6-2T

5503	5521	5543
5504	5525	5571

Class 43xx 2-6-0

6323	6343	6372	6390	7304
6337	6364	6375	6398	

'Grange' 4-6-0
6815 Frilford Grange
6868 Penrhos Grange
6874 Haughton Grange

Class 74xx 0-6-0PT
7436

Total 56

Taunton shed closed in October 1964 and the last few remaining engines transferred to Bristol Barrow Road 82E.

Taunton shed and coaler in September 1955.
W. Potter

The yard at Taunton in May 1964, five months before closure with Class 3MT 2-6-2T No 82040 (83D) on the right. K. Fairey

34

83C EXETER

Pre-Grouping Origin: GWR
Gazetteer Ref: 2 B3
Closed: 1963
Shed-Code: 83C (1949-1963)
Allocations: 1950

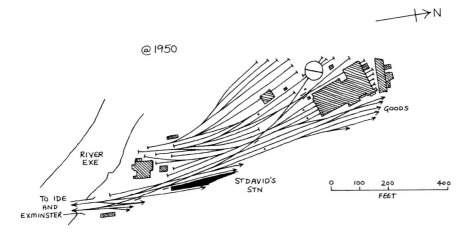

@ 1950

N

RIVER
EXE

GOODS

St DAVID'S
STN

To IDE
AND
EXMINSTER

0   100   200   400
FEET

Class 14xx 0-4-2T

1405	1435	1449	1468
1429	1440	1451	1469

Class 2021 0-6-0PT
2088

Class 2251 0-6-0
2230

Class 28xx 2-8-0
2873   3834

Class 57xx 0-6-0PT

3603	3677	5760	7761
3606	3794	7716	9647

Class 51xx 2-6-2T
4176

Class 44xx 2-6-2T
4410

Class 45xx 2-6-2T
4540   5525

'Castle' 4-6-0
5059 *Earl St Aldwyn*
5062 *Earl of Shaftesbury*

Class 43xx 2-6-0

5321	6301	6397	7316

'Hall' 4-6-0
5902 *Howick Hall*
5976 *Ashwicke Hall*
6994 *Baggrave Hall*

Class 94xx 0-6-0PT
8421   8546

Total 35

Allocations: 1959

Class 14xx 0-4-2T

1440	1451	1462	1468	1471

Class 57xx 0-6-0PT

3606	3794	7716	9629	9765

Class 51xx 2-6-2T
4117

Class 45xx 2-6-2T
4589   5546

'Hall' 4-6-0
4944 *Middleton Hall*
4948 *Northwick Hall*
4960 *Pyle Hall*
4992 *Crosby Hall*
5959 *Mawley Hall*
6965 *Thirlestaine Hall*

Class 43xx 2-6-0

5339	6385	7311	7316

Class 54xx 0-6-0PT
5412

Class 94xx 0-6-0PT
9439   9474   9497

Total 27

The shed at Exeter was also known as 'St David's' because of its close proximity to the station of the same name.

At closure in October 1963 the allocation was divided between Taunton 83B, Plymouth Laira 83D, Yeovil Town 83E, Gloucester Barnwood 85C and Oxford 81F.

A general view of Exeter in July 1957. 'Grange' 4-6-0 No 6875 Hindford Grange (83B) is nearest the camera. N. E. Preedy

Exeter St Davids shed in close-up in August 1930. IAL

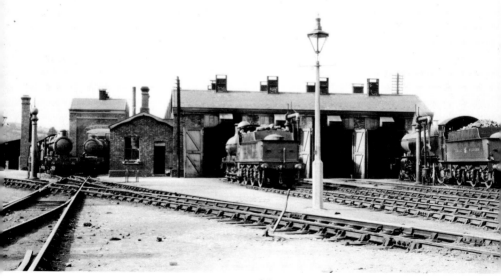

83D PLYMOUTH LAIRA

Pre-Grouping Origin: GWR
Gazetteer Ref: 1 D5
Closed: 1964
Shed-Codes: 83D (1949-1963)
84A (1963-1964)
Allocations: 1950 (83D)

@1949

To LIPSON JUNC

LAIRA JUNC

SIDINGS

N

To MOUNT GOULD JUNC

0   100   200   400
FEET

'Castle' 4-6-0
  111 *Viscount Churchill*
4032 *Queen Alexandra*
4087 *Cardigan Castle*
4088 *Dartmouth Castle*
4089 *Donnington Castle*
4097 *Kenilworth Castle*
5012 *Berry Pomeroy Castle*
5021 *Whittington Castle*
5023 *Brecon Castle*
5026 *Criccieth Castle*
5057 *Earl Waldegrave*
5058 *Earl of Clancarty*
5060 *Earl of Berkeley*
5090 *Neath Abbey*
5095 *Barbury Castle*
5098 *Clifford Castle*
7027 *Thornbury Castle*
7031 *Cromwell's Castle*

'County' 4-6-0
1006 *County of Cornwall*
1022 *County of Northampton*
1023 *County of Oxford*

Class 1361 0-6-0ST

1361	1363	1364	1365

Class 2021 0-6-0PT
2148

Class 2251 0-6-0
2258

Class 28xx 2-8-0

2875	3832	3864

Class 3150 2-6-2T

3178	3186	3187

Class 57xx 0-6-0PT

3629	3787	4679	9671	9770
3639	3790	4693	9673	
3675	4653	7762	9711	
3686	4656	8709	9716	
3705	4658	8719	9765	

'Star' 4-6-0
4054 *Princess Charlotte*

Class 44xx 2-6-2T

4407	4409

Class 45xx 2-6-2T

4517	4524	4542	4591	5567
4518	4528	4583	5540	5569

Class 47xx 2-8-0
4703

'Hall' 4-6-0
4966 *Shakenhurst Hall*
4968 *Shotton Hall*
4972 *Saint Brides Hall*
4992 *Crosby Hall*
5964 *Wolseley Hall*
5998 *Trevor Hall*
6907 *Davenham Hall*
6913 *Levens Hall*
6949 *Haberfield Hall*
7905 *Fowey Hall*
7909 *Heveningham Hall*

Class 51xx 2-6-2T
5148

37

Class 43xx 2-6-0
5318   5376   6319

'King' 4-6-0
6010 *King Charles I*
6012 *King Edward VI*
6016 *King Edward V*
6022 *King Edward III*
6023 *King Edward II*
6024 *King Edward I*
6025 *King Henry III*
6026 *King John*
6027 *King Richard I*
6029 *King Edward VIII*

Class 64xx 0-6-0PT
6406   6414   6419   6421
6407   6417   6420

'Grange' 4-6-0
6855 *Saighton Grange*
6873 *Caradoc Grange*

'Manor' 4-6-0
7801 *Anthony Manor*
7804 *Baydon Manor*
7809 *Childrey Manor*
7814 *Fringford Manor*

Class 94xx 0-6-0PT
8404

Class WD 2-8-0
90148

Total 108

Allocations: 1959 (83D)

'County' 4-6-0
1010 *County of Caernarvon*
1015 *County of Gloucester*
1021 *County of Montgomery*

Class 1361 0-6-0ST
1361   1363   1364

Class 14xx 0-4-2T
1421   1434

Class 16xx 0-6-0PT
1650

Class 28xx 2-8-0
2809   2843   2899   3862

Class 57xx 0-6-0PT
3675   3787   4658   9711
3686   3790   4679   9716

'Castle' 4-6-0
4077 *Chepstow Castle*
4087 *Cardigan Castle*
5021 *Whittington Castle*
5028 *Llantilio Castle*
5058 *Earl of Clancarty*

The interior of Laira's roundhouse in 1962 depicting two 'Castle' 4-6-0s amid four pawns, namely '45xx' 2-6-2Ts. Left to right are Nos 5564, 5568, 5000 Launceston Castle, *4087* Cardigan Castle, *5541 and 5569.*   T. Nicholls

38

5069 *Isambard Kingdom Brunel*
5075 *Wellington*
5098 *Clifford Castle*
7006 *Lydford Castle*
7022 *Hereford Castle*
7031 *Cromwell's Castle*

Class 45xx 2-6-2T
4571	4592	5531	5569
4591	5511	5567	5572

Class 47xx 2-8-0
4705

'Hall' 4-6-0
4928 *Gatacre Hall*
5972 *Olton Hall*
6913 *Levens Hall*
6921 *Borwick Hall*
6941 *Fillongley Hall*
6988 *Swithland Hall*
7905 *Fowey Hall*

Class 51xx 2-6-2T
5106	5148	5175

'King' 4-6-0
6004 *King George III*
6007 *King William III*
6010 *King Charles I*
6016 *King Edward V*
6021 *King Richard II*
6025 *King Henry III*
6026 *King John*
6027 *King Richard I*
6029 *King Edward VIII*

The 'new' shed at Laira in July 1960 under diesel occupation. To the right of the view the roundhouse entrance can just be seen.   R. C. Riley

Class 43xx 2-6-0
6301	6319	7333	7335

Class 64xx 0-6-0PT
6402	6414	6420
6406	6419	6421

'Grange' 4-6-0
6849 *Walton Grange*
6850 *Cleeve Grange*
6863 *Dolhywel Grange*
6871 *Bourton Grange*
6873 *Caradoc Grange*

'Manor' 4-6-0
7812 *Erlestoke Manor*
7813 *Freshford Manor*
7820 *Dinmore Manor*

Class 94xx 0-6-0PT
8422	9433	9467

Total 81

Laira's 1950 allocation lists no fewer than seven different main line named classes and indicates the past importance of the depot.

The shed closed in April 1964 and the last two locos departed for Taunton 83B.

83E ST BLAZEY

Pre-Grouping Origin: GWR
Gazetteer Ref: 1 D3
Closed: 1962
Shed-Code: 83E (1949-1962)
Allocations: 1950

Class 14xx 0-4-2T
1419

Class 16xx 0-6-0PT
1626

Class 2021 0-6-0PT
2050

Class 2181 0-6-0PT
2182

Class 57xx 0-6-0PT
3635	7715	9655
7709	8783	9755

Class 42xx 2-8-0T
4215	4298

Class 45xx 2-6-2T
4503	4526	4559	4569	5502
4505	4529	4565	4570	5519
4516	4552	4568	4598	5531

'Hall' 4-6-0
4940 *Ludford Hall*
5926 *Grotrian Hall*

Class 43xx 2-6-0
6330	6356

Class 74xx 0-6-0PT
7446

Total 32

Allocations: 1959

Class 14xx 0-4-2T
1419

Class 16xx 0-6-0PT
1624	1626	1664

Class 57xx 0-6-0PT
3635	7709	8702	8733	9673
3705	7715	8719	9655	9755

Class 51xx 2-6-2T
4167	5193

Class 42xx 2-8-0T
4206	4294

Class 45xx 2-6-2T
4547	4564	4585	5539
4552	4565	5519	5551
4559	4569	5523	5557

'Hall' 4-6-0
4906 *Bradfield Hall*
6931 *Aldborough Hall*

Class 43xx 2-6-0
6397

'Grange' 4-6-0
6814 *Enborne Grange*

Class 74xx 0-6-0PT
7446

St Blazey shed in October 1958. T. Nicholls

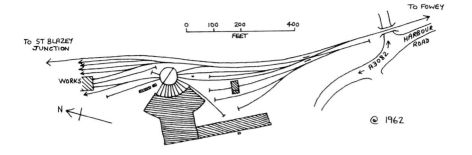

To ST BLAZEY JUNCTION

WORKS

N

TO FOWEY

HARBOUR ROAD

← A3082 ↑

0   100   200   400
FEET

@ 1962

'Manor' 4-6-0
7816 *Frilsham Manor*

Class 94xx 0-6-0PT
8485

Total 37

St Blazey closed in April 1962 and the few remaining locos transferred to Neath 87A, Laira 83D and Machynlleth 89C.

Looking south across St Blazey's roads in 1954 with Class 45xx 2-6-2T No 4568 (83E) to the fore.
Photomatic

83F TRURO

Pre-Grouping Origin: GWR
Gazetteer Ref: 1 E1
Closed: 1962
Shed-Code: 83F (1949-1962)
Allocations: 1950

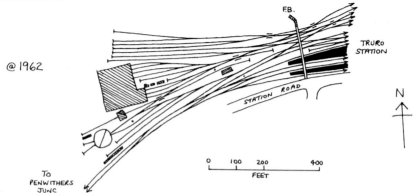

@ 1962

'County' 4-6-0
1013 *County of Dorset*

Class 1501 0-6-0PT
1782

Class 2021 0-6-0PT
2097

Class 51xx 2-6-2T
4167

Class 45xx 2-6-2T

4504	4561	5500	5537
4523	4588	5515	5562
4554	4589	5526	

'Hall' 4-6-0
4906 *Bradfield Hall*
4936 *Kinlet Hall*
6931 *Aldborough Hall*

Class 57xx 0-6-0PT
5779

Class 43xx 2-6-0
6373

'Grange' 4-6-0
6872 *Crawley Grange*

Class 74xx 0-6-0PT
7422

Class 94xx 0-6-0PT
8412

Total 23

Allocations: 1959

'County' 4-6-0
1007 *County of Brecknock*
1023 *County of Oxford*

Class 57xx 0-6-0PT
3702

Class 45xx 2-6-2T

4508	4587	5515	5537	5559
4574	5500	5533	5552	5562

Class 43xx 2-6-0
5376   6300

'Grange' 4-6-0
6805 *Broughton Grange*
6823 *Oakley Grange*
6828 *Trellech Grange*
6832 *Brockton Grange*
6855 *Saighton Grange*
6879 *Overton Grange*

'Hall' 4-6-0
6911 *Holker Hall*

'Manor' 4-6-0
7823 *Hook Norton Manor*

Class 94xx 0-6-0PT

8412	8421	8486	9434

Total 27

Truro's last two locomotives were transferred to Taunton 83B and Westbury 82D in March 1962.

42

Truro shed as viewed from the running lines in 1952. Real Photos

Looking west to Truro MPD from the Station Road footbridge in 1922. LGRP, courtesy David & Charles

83G PENZANCE

Pre-Grouping Origin: GWR
Gazetteer Ref: 1 F4
Closed: 1962
Shed-Code: 83G (1949-1962)
Allocations: 1950

'County' 4-6-0
1004 *County of Somerset*

'Castle' 4-6-0
4090 *Dorchester Castle*

Class 45xx 2-6-2T
4500	4525	4545	4566
4509	4537	4548	4574

'Hall' 4-6-0
4946 *Moseley Hall*
4947 *Nanhoran Hall*
4965 *Rood Ashton Hall*
5915 *Trentham Hall*
5969 *Honington Hall*
6911 *Holker Hall*

Class 43xx 2-6-0
6318   6354

'Grange' 4-6-0
6800 *Arlington Grange*
6801 *Aylburton Grange*
6806 *Blackwell Grange*
6808 *Beenham Grange*
6809 *Burghclere Grange*
6817 *Gwenddwr Grange*
6825 *Llanvair Grange*
6826 *Nannerth Grange*
6838 *Goodmoor Grange*
6869 *Resolven Grange*

Class 94xx 0-6-0PT
8409

Class 57xx 0-6-0PT
9717

Total 30

Allocations: 1959

'County' 4-6-0
1002 *County of Berks*
1006 *County of Cornwall*
1008 *County of Cardigan*
1018 *County of Leicester*

'Castle' 4-6-0
4095 *Harlech Castle*
5020 *Trematon Castle*

Class 51xx 2-6-2T
4136

Class 45xx 2-6-2T
4563	4570	4588
4566	4577	5524

'Hall' 4-6-0
4908 *Broome Hall*
4931 *Hanbury Hall*
4950 *Patshull Hall*
4976 *Warfield Hall*
5934 *Kneller Hall*
7925 *Westol Hall*

'Grange' 4-6-0
6800 *Arlington Grange*
6801 *Aylburton Grange*
6808 *Beenham Grange*
6816 *Frankton Grange*
6824 *Ashley Grange*
6825 *Llanvair Grange*
6826 *Nannerth Grange*
6837 *Forthampton Grange*
6845 *Paviland Grange*
6860 *Aberporth Grange*
6870 *Bodicote Grange*
6875 *Hindford Grange*

Class 94xx 0-6-0PT
8409   8473

Class 57xx 0-6-0PT
9748

Total 34

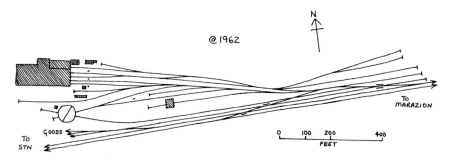

@ 1962

N

To
MARAZION

GOODS
To
STN

0   100   200   400
FEET

A pair of Penzance's 'Grange' allocation at the shed in May 1957. Left is No 6845 Paviland Grange *and right 6837* Forthampton Grange. T. Wright

Penzance shed was closed in September 1962 and the last few remaining locomotives went to Neyland 87H and Duffryn Yard 87B.

An overall view of Penzance shed on a dismal day in 1950. LGRP, courtesy David & Charles

84A WOLVERHAMPTON STAFFORD ROAD

Pre-Grouping Origin: GWR
Gazetteer Ref: 15 F3
Closed: 1963
Shed-Code: 84A (1949-1963)
Allocations: 1950

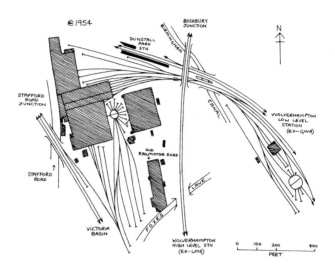

'County' 4-6-0
1016 *County of Hants*
1017 *County of Hereford*
1024 *County of Pembroke*
1025 *County of Radnor*
1029 *County of Worcester*

Class 14xx 0-4-2T
1410

Class 2021 0-6-0PT
2061   2095   2109

Class 31xx 2-6-2T
3102   3104

Class 3150 2-6-2T
3160

Class 57xx 0-6-0PT
3615   3778   5739   8705   8734
3756   5701   5780   8726   9621

'Castle' 4-6-0
4000 *North Star*
5008 *Raglan Castle*
5010 *Restormel Castle*
5015 *Kingswear Castle*
5022 *Wigmore Castle*

5031 *Totnes Castle*
5053 *Earl Cairns*
5070 *Sir Daniel Gooch*
5088 *Llanthony Abbey*
7026 *Tenby Castle*

'Star' 4-6-0
4018 *Knight of the Grand Cross*
4031 *Queen Mary*
4049 *Princess Maud*
4053 *Princess Alexandra*
4058 *Princess Augusta*
4060 *Princess Eugenie*

Class 51xx 2-6-2T
4103   4108   5143
4105   4115   5151

Class 43xx 2-6-0
4337   6321   6391   7315

'Hall' 4-6-0
4960 *Pyle Hall*
5942 *Doldowlod Hall*
5944 *Ickenham Hall*
5995 *Wick Hall*
6901 *Arley Hall*
6924 *Grantley Hall*
6964 *Thornbridge Hall*
7915 *Mear Hall*

46

'King' 4-6-0
6004 *King George III*
6005 *King George II*
6006 *King George I*
6008 *King James II*
6011 *King James I*
6020 *King Henry IV*

'Grange' 4-6-0
6812 *Chesford Grange*
6848 *Toddington Grange*

Class 94xx 0-6-0PT
8411   8462

Total 66

Allocations: 1959

Class 57xx 0-6-0PT

3615	3756	3792	8796
3664	3778	8726	8798

Class 51xx 2-6-2T

4161	5151	5187

'Hall' 4-6-0
4901 *Adderley Hall*
4986 *Aston Hall*
4990 *Clifton Hall*
5900 *Hinderton Hall*
5926 *Grotrian Hall*
6975 *Capesthorne Hall*

'Castle' 4-6-0
5019 *Treago Castle*
5022 *Wigmore Castle*
5026 *Criccieth Castle*

Looking west to the corrugated structures at Stafford Road in May 1958. W. Potter

5031 *Totnes Castle*
5045 *Earl of Dudley*
5046 *Earl Cawdor*
5047 *Earl of Dartmouth*
5059 *Earl St Aldwyn*
5063 *Earl Baldwin*
5070 *Sir Daniel Gooch*
5072 *Hurricane*
5088 *Llanthony Abbey*
5089 *Westminster Abbey*
7026 *Tenby Castle*

'King' 4-6-0
6001 *King Edward VII*
6005 *King George II*
6006 *King George I*
6008 *King James II*
6011 *King James I*
6014 *King Henry VII*
6017 *King Edward IV*
6020 *King Henry IV*

Class 64xx 0-6-0PT
6418   6422

Class 94xx 0-6-0PT

8411	8426	9435
8425	9428	9496

Total 47

Stafford Road shed was closed in September 1963 and the remaining locos went to Oxley 2B (ex-84B).

47

84B WOLVERHAMPTON OXLEY

Pre-Grouping Origin: GWR
Gazetteer Ref: 15 F3
Closed: 1967
Shed-Codes: 84B (1949-1963)
2B (1963-1967)
Allocations: 1950 (84B)

Class 28xx 2-8-0

2825	2830	2832	2833	2854

Class ROD 2-8-0

3031	3033

Class 57xx 0-6-0PT

3744	5748	8798	9739	9768
3745	7759	9714	9742	9769
3792	7796	9715	9747	
3793	7797	9730	9752	

Class 47xx 2-8-0
4708

'Hall' 4-6-0
4955 *Plaspower Hall*
4991 *Cobham Hall*
5921 *Bingley Hall*
5945 *Leckhampton Hall*
5991 *Gresham Hall*
6920 *Barningham Hall*
6956 *Mottram Hall*
6967 *Willesley Hall*
6975 *Capesthorne Hall*

Class 43xx 2-6-0

5309	5386	6361	9312
5313	5390	6362	9414
5379	6335	7311	

Class 56xx 0-6-2T

5606	5657	6600	6610	6640
5624	5684	6609	6638	6645

'Grange' 4-6-0
6856 *Stowe Grange*
6862 *Derwent Grange*
6879 *Overton Grange*

Class 72xx 2-8-2T

7207	7226	7227	7238	7243

Class 94xx 0-6-0PT

8417	9408

Class WD 2-8-0
90141

Total 67

Allocations: 1959 (84B)

Class 28xx 2-8-0

2841	2859	3813	3837	3863

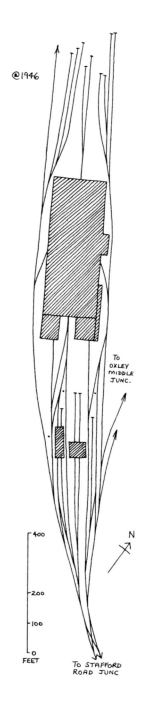

@1946

To
OXLEY
MIDDLE
JUNC.

N

400
200
100
0
FEET

To STAFFORD
ROAD JUNC

48

2850	2888	3820	3846	3865	
2857	3802	3829	3861		

Class 57xx 0-6-0PT

3698	7759	9739	9752	9768

'Hall' 4-6-0
4951 *Pendeford Hall*
4957 *Postlip Hall*
4963 *Rignall Hall*
4966 *Shakenhurst Hall*
4984 *Albrighton Hall*
4997 *Elton Hall*
5916 *Trinity Hall*
5919 *Worlsey Hall*
5944 *Ickenham Hall*
5965 *Woollas Hall*
5985 *Mostyn Hall*
5991 *Gresham Hall*
5995 *Wick Hall*
6907 *Davenham Hall*
6925 *Hackness Hall*
6934 *Beachamwell Hall*
7915 *Mere Hall*

Class 43xx 2-6-0

6353	7339	7341

Class 56xx 0-6-2T

6640	6645

'Grange' 4-6-0
6806 *Blackwell Grange*
6817 *Gwenddwr Grange*
6839 *Hewell Grange*

6857 *Tudor Grange*
6862 *Derwent Grange*

Class 72xx 2-8-2T
7247

'Manor' 4-6-0
7818 *Granville Manor*

Class 94xx 0-6-0PT

8428	8462	9408

Total 51

Allocations: 1965 (2B)

Class 57xx 0-6-0PT

3605	3776	3792	9658
3631	3782	8767	9776
3744	3788	9640	

The interior of Oxley depot in April 1962. Left to right are Nos 3631, 9435, 9623, 5606, 9768 and 6925 Hackness Hall. W. T. Stubbs

Class 51xx 2-6-2T
4148   4165   4176

'Grange' 4-6-0
6803 *Bucklebury Grange*
6823 *Oakley Grange*
6827 *Llanfrechfa Grange*
6830 *Buckenhill Grange*
6831 *Bearley Grange*
6833 *Calcot Grange*
6851 *Hurst Grange*
6854 *Roundhill Grange*
6855 *Saighton Grange*
6857 *Tudor Grange*
6858 *Woolston Grange*
6862 *Derwent Grange*
6864 *Dymock Grange*
6870 *Bodicote Grange*
6871 *Bourton Grange*

'Manor' 4-6-0
7820 *Dinmore Manor*
7821 *Ditcheat Manor*

Class 5MT 2-6-0
42946   42957   42983

Class 5MT 4-6-0

44691	44812	44919	45186	45283
44805	44841	45006	45263	
44808	44856	45040	45272	

Class 8F 2-8-0

48016	48120	48475	48738	48755

Class 5MT 4-6-0

73013	73014	73019	73028

Looking north-west to the coaler at Oxley in June 1953 with the shed buildings in the background.
W. Potter

Class 4MT 2-6-0
76022

Class 2MT 2-6-0
78008

Total 58

Oxley became London Midland Region property in September 1963 and was recoded 2B.

At closure in March 1967, the bulk of the remaining engines went to Crewe South 5B but others transferred to Chester 6A, Stoke 5D and Wigan Springs Branch 8F.

84C BANBURY

Pre-Grouping Origin: GWR
Gazetteer Ref: 10 C4
Closed: 1966
Shed-Codes: 84C (1949-1963)
2D (1963-1966)
Allocations: 1950 (84C)

Class 14xx 0-4-2T
1401	1411	1458

Class 2251 0-6-0
2256	2295	3216	3218

Class 28xx 2-8-0
2805	2863	2897	3819	3849
2816	2869	2898	3820	3861
2847	2883	2899	3829	3863
2853	2886	3802	3831	3865

'Saint' 4-6-0
2981 *Ivanhoe*

Class ROD 2-8-0
3020	3043

Class 57xx 0-6-0PT
3630	4631	5724	8729	9782
3694	4646	7763	8787	

Class 51xx 2-6-2T
4149

Class 43xx 2-6-0
5317	5332	6342
5324	5361	6390

Class 54xx 0-6-0PT
5404	5407	5417	5424

'Hall' 4-6-0
5930 *Hannington Hall*
5967 *Bickmarsh Hall*
6906 *Chicheley Hall*
6929 *Whorlton Hall*
6979 *Helperly Hall*

Class 64xx 0-6-0PT
6418

Class 56xx 0-6-2T
6696

'Grange' 4-6-0
6803 *Bucklebury Grange*
6816 *Frankton Grange*
6819 *Highnam Grange*
6835 *Eastham Grange*
6839 *Hewell Grange*
6854 *Roundhill Grange*

'Manor' 4-6-0
7805 *Broome Manor*
7806 *Cockington Manor*
7811 *Dunley Manor*

Class 94xx 0-6-0PT
8400	8405	8407	8459

Total 70

A 'Castle' 4-6-0 No 5046 Earl Cawdor *(84A) is on
the left of this 1962 view of Banbury shed.*   K. Fairey

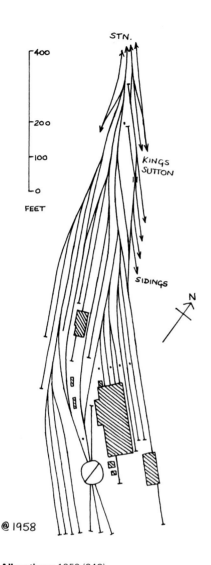

@ 1958

STN.

KINGS
SUTTON

SIDINGS

N

400

200

100

0

FEET

'Hall' 4-6-0
4924 *Eydon Hall*
4942 *Maindy Hall*
4964 *Rodwell Hall*
5921 *Bingley Hall*
5930 *Hannington Hall*
5947 *Saint Benet's Hall*
5989 *Cransley Hall*
6906 *Chicheley Hall*
6929 *Whorlton Hall*
6949 *Haberfield Hall*
6976 *Graythwaite Hall*
6979 *Helperly Hall*

Class 43xx 2-6-0

5337	6311	6387	7308
5375	6331	7305	7315

Class 54xx 0-6-0PT

5407	5420	5424

Class 94xx 0-6-0PT

8452	9449

Class WD 2-8-0

90148	90313	90585

Class 9F 2-10-0

92221	92223	92225	92227	92250
92222	92224	92226	92228	

Total 52

Allocations: 1965 (2D)

Class 2251 0-6-0
2210

Class 51xx 2-6-2T
4154

'Hall' 4-6-0
6903 *Belmont Hall*
6916 *Misterton Hall*
6917 *Oldlands Hall*
6934 *Beachamwell Hall*
6951 *Impney Hall*
6952 *Kimberley Hall*
6976 *Graythwaite Hall*
6980 *Llanrumney Hall*
7912 *Little Linford Hall*

Class 9F 2-10-0

92004	92129	92218	92228
92028	92203	92224	92234
92128	92213	92227	92247

Total 23

Banbury shed became London Midland Region property in September 1963 and was allocated the code 2D.

The depot closed in October 1966 and its 12 remaining engines were transferred to no fewer than eight other London Midland sheds.

Allocations: 1959 (84C)

Class 2251 0-6-0

2211	2234	2270
2230	2256	2297

Class 28xx 2-8-0

2816	2890	3856	3858

Class 57xx 0-6-0PT

3646	7761

Class 51xx 2-6-2T

4149	5152	5170

84D LEAMINGTON SPA

Pre-Grouping Origin: GWR
Gazetteer Ref: 10 B5
Closed: 1965
Shed-Codes: 84D (1949-1963)
2L (1963-1965)
Allocations: 1950 (84D)

'Saint' 4-6-0
2933 *Bilbury Court*

Class 57xx 0-6-0PT
3631   7702   9740

Class 51xx 2-6-2T
4102   4171   5144   5163   5192
4112   5104   5161   5185   5194

Class 56xx 0-6-2T
5634   6625   6632   6657   6697

'Hall' 4-6-0
5954 *Faendre Hall*

'Grange' 4-6-0
6833 *Calcot Grange*

Class 72xx 2-8-2T
7208   7218   7237

'Manor' 4-6-0
7810 *Draycott Manor*

Class 81xx 2-6-2T
8100   8109

Class 94xx 0-6-0PT
8454

Class WD 2-8-0
90685

Total 29

Allocations: 1959 (84D)

Class 57xx 0-6-2PT
3619   3624   3631   7702

Class 51xx 2-6-2T
4103   4118   4171   5184
4112   4162   5101

Class 56xx 0-6-2T
6657   6697

Class 81xx 2-6-2T
8100   8109

Class 2 2-6-2T
41227   41228   41285

Class 4 2-6-4T
42566

Class WD 2-8-0
90483

Total 20

Allocations: 1965 (2L)

Class 56xx 0-6-2T
6644   6671   6697

Class 2MT 2-6-0
46428   46442   46457   46470   46505

Class 5MT 4-6-0
73026   73066   73069   73156

Class 4MT 2-6-4T
80072

Total 13

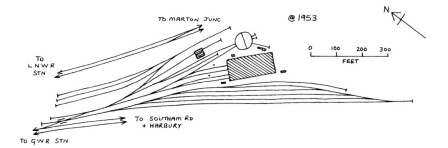

@ 1953

Leamington transferred to the London Midland Region's control in September 1963 and assumed the code 2L.
The shed closed in June 1965 and the bulk of the engines went to Tyseley 2A (ex-84E).

Leamington Spa shed in 1962. K. Fairey

A south-easterly view of the Leamington site in 1954. W. Potter

84E TYSELEY

Pre-Grouping Origin: GWR
Gazetteer Ref: 15 G5
Closed: 1966
Shed-Codes: 84E (1949-1963)
2A (1963-1966)
Allocations: 1950 (84E)

Class 2251 0-6-0

2203	2238	2257	2296

Class 28xx 2-8-0

2848	2849	2867	3837

'Saint' 4-6-0
2932 Ashton Court

Class ROD 2-8-0
3016

Class 31xx 2-6-2T
3101

Class 3150 2-6-2T

3151	3180

Class 57xx 0-6-0PT

3624	3673	4683	7735	9680
3625	3689	5700	7758	9682
3650	3693	5712	8700	9724
3653	3743	5736	8784	9733
3657	3751	5738	9608	9748
3658	3769	5745	9610	9753
3660	4605	5790	9614	9793
3664	4648	7713	9635	9798

Class 51xx 2-6-2T

4101	4147	4172	5166	5188
4106	4157	5102	5171	5190
4107	4159	5106	5175	5198
4110	4165	5152	5177	
4111	4166	5156	5182	
4116	4170	5164	5187	

'Hall' 4-6-0
4924 Eydon Hall
4959 Purley Hall
4964 Rodwell Hall
4980 Wrottesley Hall
5907 Marble Hall
5909 Newton Hall
5916 Trinity Hall
5927 Guild Hall
5950 Wardley Hall
5993 Kirby Hall
5997 Sparkford Hall
6904 Charfield Hall
6942 Eshton Hall
6971 Athelhampton Hall
7912 Little Linford Hall
7913 Little Wyrley Hall
7918 Rhose Wood Hall

Class 43xx 2-6-0

5333	5369	6336
5346	5370	7317

Class 56xx 0-6-2T

6611	6630

'Grange' 4-6-0
6843 Poulton Grange
6847 Tidmarsh Grange
6853 Morehampton Grange
6858 Woolston Grange
6866 Morfa Grange

Class 74xx 0-6-0PT
7438

*Looking south to Tyseley depot in 1949 with 'Saint'
4-6-0 No 2903 Lady of Lyons (84E) prominent. This
loco was withdrawn from service in November
1949.* Real Photos

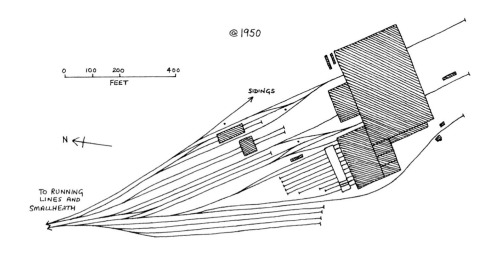

@ 1950

SIDINGS

N ←

TO RUNNING
LINES AND
SMALLHEATH

| 0 | 100 | 200 | 400 |
FEET

'Manor' 4-6-0
7800 Torquay Manor

Class 81xx 2-6-2T
8108

Class 94xx 0-6-0PT
8410   8415   8452

Class 90xx 4-4-0
9008   9010

Total 118

Allocations: 1959 (84E)

Class 2251 0-6-0
2238   2257   2267

Class 28xx 2-8-0
2849   2856   2885   2897   3839
2851   2882   2886   3831

Class 57xx 0-6-0PT
3625   4648   8700   9682   9798
3657   5745   8713   9724
3660   7713   9614   9727
3673   7735   9635   9733
3693   7763   9680   9753

Class 51xx 2-6-2T
4111   4155   4172   5192
4126   4170   5163

'Hall' 4-6-0
4974 Talgarth Hall
4982 Acton Hall
5912 Queen's Hall
5927 Guild Hall
6904 Charfield Hall
6971 Athelhampton Hall
7908 Henshall Hall
7912 Little Linford Hall
7918 Rhose Wood Hall

Class 43xx 2-6-0
5369   5378   6399
5370   6357   7317

Class 56xx 0-6-2T
5658   6631   6668

Class 61xx 2-6-2T
6116   6139   6160

'Grange' 4-6-0
6853 Morehampton Grange
6861 Crynant Grange
6866 Morfa Grange

Class 74xx 0-6-0PT
7420

'Manor' 4-6-0
7821 *Ditcheat Manor*

Class 81xx 2-6-2T
8108

Class 94xx 0-6-0PT
8415   8468   9432

Total 70

Allocations: 1965 (2A)

Class 57xx 0-6-0PT
3625   4635   9753   9774

Class 51xx 2-6-2T
4111   4125   4155   4158   4178

Class 56xx 0-6-2T
5606   5684   6667   6681
5658   6633   6668

'Hall' 4-6-0
5988 *Bostock Hall*
6922 *Burton Hall*
6926 *Holkham Hall*
6930 *Aldersey Hall*
6964 *Thornbridge Hall*
7908 *Henshall Hall*
7915 *Mere Hall*
7929 *Wyke Hall*

'Grange' 4-6-0
6853 *Morehampton Grange*
6861 *Crynant Grange*

6866 *Morfa Grange*
6879 *Overton Grange*

Class 81xx 2-6-2T
8109

Class 8F 2-8-0
48415   48474

Class 9F 2-10-0
92001   92118   92212   92217
92002   92204   92215   92223

Total 39

Tyseley became part of the London Midland Region in September 1963 and was issued the code 2A.

The shed had the distinction of housing the last standard gauge ex-GWR locos in service, namely 4646, 4696 and 9774 (all '57xx' class).

At closure in November 1966, the bulk of the remaining locos (all 'Black 5', '8F' and '9F' types) were moved to Oxley 2B, Croes Newydd 6C, Shrewsbury 6D and Carnforth 10A.

Much of the shed remains and forms the basis for the Birmingham Railway Museum. Understandably, the accent is GWR and many preserved locos are both stored and operated.

The interior of Tyseley in January 1957 with four 2-6-2T types grouped around the turntable. Note the numerical sequence left to right: Nos 3101, 4116, 5198 and 6166 (all 84E).   H. C. Casserley

84F STOURBRIDGE

Origin: GWR (1926)
Gazetteer Ref: 15 G3
Closed: 1966
Shed-Codes: 84F (1949-1963)
2C (1963-1966)
Allocations: 1950 (84F)

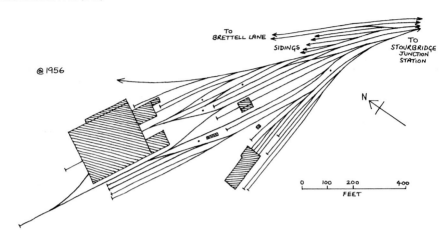

Class 14xx 0-4-2T
1414	1438

Class 16xx 0-6-OPT
1621

Class 2021 0-6-OPT
2090	2107

Class 2181 0-6-OPT
2185	2186	2187	2189

Class 2251 0-6-0
2246	2270	2279

Class 28xx 2-8-0
2852	2857	2885	3827
2856	2874	3821	

Class 57xx 0-6-OPT
3649	4696	5795	8792	9767
3667	5719	7705	8797	
3740	5726	8704	9613	
4638	5754	8742	9636	
4687	5794	8791	9741	

Class 51xx 2-6-2T
4104	5105	5147	5170	5196
4146	5107	5155	5180	5197
4150	5122	5160	5189	5199
4173	5134	5165	5191	
5101	5136	5167	5193	

Class 43xx 2-6-0
5300	6332

Class 56xx 0-6-2T
5651	6617	6667	6677
5658	6646	6674	6678

'Grange' 4-6-0
6828 *Trellech Grange*
6857 *Tudor Grange*

Class 74xx 0-6-OPT
7402	7429	7432	7448
7428	7430	7435	7449

Class 94xx 0-6-OPT
8418	8419

Total 85

Allocations: 1959 (84F)

Class 16xx 0-6-OPT
1619	1621

Class 28xx 2-8-0
2804	2823	2853	3821	3825

Class 57xx 0-6-OPT
3649	3743	5754	8797	9767
3658	3745	5795	9613	9782
3667	4646	8704	9624	

Stourbridge shed and yard in June 1953.
N. E. Preedy

3710	4687	8742	9636
3729	4696	8792	9719

Class 51xx 2-6-2T

4104	4146	4173	5189
4140	4168	5176	5199

Class 43xx 2-6-0

6317	6332	6340	6349	6367

Class 64xx 0-6-0PT

6401	6403

Class 56xx 0-6-2T

6604	6646	6674	6678	6692
6609	6667	6677	6683	

'Grange' 4-6-0
6803 *Bucklebury Grange*

'Hall' 4-6-0
6930 *Aldersey Hall*
6987 *Shervington Hall*

Class 74xx 0-6-0PT

7429	7432	7441	7448
7430	7435	7447	7449

Total 64

Allocations: 1965 (2C)

Class 57xx 0-6-0PT

3607	4665	9608	9641	9733
3619	4696	9613	9646	
3658	8718	9614	9724	

Class 51xx 2-6-2T

4147	4168	4175

Class 61xx 2-6-2T
6129

Class 56xx 0-6-2T

6656	6679	6683	6692

Class 8F 2-8-0

48330	48410	48424	48460
48353	48412	48450	48468
48402	48417	48459	48762

Total 33

Stourbridge shed became London Midland Region property in September 1963 and began using the 2C code.

The shed closed in July 1966 and the bulk of remaining locomotives went to Tyseley 2A, Oxley 2B, Croes Newydd 6C and Rose Grove 10F.

Inside the roundhouse at Stourbridge in 1962 with 'WD' class 2-8-0 No 90148 (84C) rubbing shoulders with various 0-6-0PTs.   W. T. Stubbs

84G SHREWSBURY

Pre-Grouping Origin: GWR/LNWR Joint
Gazetteer Ref: 15 E1
Closed: 1967
Shed-Codes: 4A (1948-1949)
84G (1949-1960)
89A (1960-1963)
6D (1963-1967)
Allocations: 1950 (84G)

Class 2251 0-6-0

2228	2231	2234	3217
2229	2233	2235	

Class 2721 0-6-0PT
2744

Class 28xx 2-8-0
2841

Class 57xx 0-6-0PT

3602	3788	4672	9672
3702	4602	9656	9719
3782	4623	9657	

'Star' 4-6-0
4040 *Queen Boadicea*
4044 *Prince George*
4046 *Princess Mary*
4052 *Princess Beatrice*
4061 *Glastonbury Abbey*

Class 51xx 2-6-2T

4118	5154	5168

'Hall' 4-6-0
4904 *Binnegar Hall*
4919 *Donnington Hall*
5981 *Frensham Hall*
5994 *Roydon Hall*
6963 *Throwley Hall*
6976 *Graythwaite Hall*
6980 *Llanrumney Hall*

'Castle' 4-6-0
5032 *Usk Castle*
5050 *Earl of St Germans*
5061 *Earl of Birkenhead*
5064 *Bishops Castle*
5073 *Blenheim*
5086 *Viscount Horne*
5097 *Sarum Castle*
7035 *Ogmore Castle*

Class 56xx 0-6-2T

5642	5673	6606	6633	6683

Class 43xx 2-6-0

6307	6338	6348	7319

Class 3MT 2-6-2T

40005	40008	40048	40058

Class 1F 0-6-0T
41725

Class 3F 0-6-0

43357	43570	43600	43757
43394	43581	43679	43760

Class 5MT 4-6-0

44835	45145	45245	45318	45406
44908	45180	45281	45330	45422
45112	45183	45283	45384	45436
45143	45190	45298	45400	

Sentinel 0-4-0T
47183

Class 8F 2-8-0

48207	48308	48347	48373	48478
48307	48328	48369	48474	48688

Class 7F 0-8-0

48901	48945	49138	49276	49440

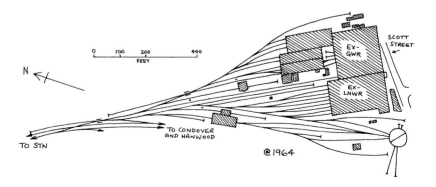

Class 3F 0-6-0
52414   52428   52525   52551

Class 0F 0-4-0ST
56027

Class 2F 0-6-0
58211   58322   58330
58213   58327   58333

Class 2F 0-6-2T
58881   58904

Class WD 2-8-0
90110   90123   90535   90561
90113   90366   90548

Total 120

Allocations: 1959 (84G)

'County' 4-6-0
1003 County of Wilts
1013 County of Dorset
1016 County of Hants
1017 County of Hereford
1022 County of Northampton
1025 County of Radnor
1026 County of Salop

Class SHT 0-4-0ST
1142

Class 2251 0-6-0
2210   2289

Class 94xx 0-6-0PT
3400   8449   9470   9472   9498

The ex-GWR side of Shrewsbury shed in June 1961. W. Potter

Class 57xx 0-6-0PT
3602   3782   4623   5791   9656
3769   3788   4693   7797   9657

Class 42xx 2-8-0T
4212

'Hall' 4-6-0
4904 Binnegar Hall
4912 Berrington Hall
4913 Baglan Hall
4918 Dartington Hall
4968 Shotton Hall
5968 Cory Hall
6916 Misterton Hall
6926 Holkham Hall
6944 Fledborough Hall
6956 Mottram Hall
6964 Thornbridge Hall
6980 Llanrumney Hall
6998 Burton Agnes Hall
7921 Edstone Hall
7922 Salford Hall

'Castle' 4-6-0
5001 Llandovery Castle
5038 Morlais Castle
5050 Earl of St Germans
5097 Sarum Castle

61

Class 43xx 2-6-0

5319	6303	7309	7336
5331	6395	7329	9308

Class 56xx 0-6-2T

5634	5690	6698

'Manor' 4-6-0
7811 *Dunley Manor*
7828 *Odney Manor*

Class 4 2-6-4T

42320	42372	42418
42362	42395	42420

Class 5 4-6-0

44835	45145	45281	45298	45422
45143	45190	45283	45406	

Class 8F 2-8-0

48110	48347	48460	48660	48739
48172	48354	48468	48707	
48307	48369	48474	48724	
48328	48438	48478	48738	

Class 7F 0-8-0
49243

Class 5 4-6-0

73034	73037	73092	73095
73035	73090	73093	73096
73036	73091	73094	73097

Class WD 2-8-0

90261	90716

Total 105

Allocations: 1965 (6D)

Class 57xx 0-6-0PT

3709	3754	9657

'Manor' 4-6-0
7801 *Anthony Manor*
7802 *Bradley Manor*
7812 *Erlestoke Manor*
7819 *Hinton Manor*
7822 *Foxcote Manor*

7827 *Lydham Manor*
7828 *Odney Manor*

Class 2MT 2-6-2T

41207	41209	41304

Class 2MT 2-6-0

46510	46511	46519

Class 8F 2-8-0

48122	48404	48436
48345	48418	48471

Class 5MT 4-6-0

73000	73035	73053	73071	73095
73025	73036	73067	73090	73097
73034	73050	73070	73094	73167

Class 4MT 4-6-0

75014	75038	75053	75063

Class 4MT 2-6-4T

80048	80100	80135	80136

Total 45

The unusual combination of classes in the allocations was the result of the shed's previous dual identity. The Western Region was given complete control when engines from both stables were issued with 84G codes in 1949. As far as the period 1948-49 is concerned, the ex-LMS locos continued with 4A identities whilst their fate was decided.

The effects of regional reorganisation in October 1960 found Shrewsbury recoded 89A. Although not given official status until January 1961, many of the depot's engines were sporting the new codes in the former month.

The London Midland Region took control of the shed in September 1963 and allocated the code 6D.

The depot closed in March 1967 and the remaining stock was dispersed to 10 other depots.

Shrewsbury (ex-LMS 4A) which stood west of the GWR portion, on the same day in 1961. Note that the LMS types are in predominance here whilst the GWR engines occupy the other side (see accompanying view). W. Potter

84H WELLINGTON

Pre-Grouping Origin: GWR
Gazetteer Ref: 15 E2
Closed: 1964
Shed-Codes: 84H (1949-1963)
2M (1963-1964)
Allocations: 1950 (84H)

Class 16xx 0-6-0PT
1619

Class 2021 0-6-0PT
2030

Class 57xx 0-6-0PT

3613	3749	5758	9630
3687	3760	7754	9639
3732	3775	9624	

Class 51xx 2-6-2T

4154	5125	5138	5178
5109	5137	5139	

Class 44xx 2-6-2T

4400	4401	4403	4406

Total 24

Allocations: 1959 (84H)

Class 57xx 0-6-0PT

3626	3744	9630	9741
3732	4605	9639	9774

Class 51xx 2-6-2T

4110	4120	4158	5167

Class 3 2-6-2T

82004	82006	82009

Total 15

Wellington became London Midland Region property in September 1963 and was recoded 2M.

At closure in August 1964, the remaining engines were transferred to Oxley 2B, Croes Newydd 6C, Tyseley 2A and Stourbridge 2C.

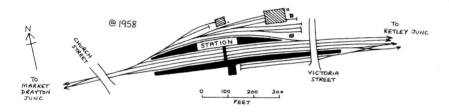

Wellington shed in July 1957 as viewed from the station.   J. Peden

84J CROES NEWYDD

Pre-Grouping Origin: GWR
Gazetteer Ref: 20 E4
Closed: 1967
Shed-Codes: 84J (1949-1960)
89B (1960-1963)
6C (1963-1967)
Allocations: 1950 (84J)

Class 14xx 0-4-2T
1416	1457	1473	5810	5811

Class 16xx 0-6-0PT
1624

Class 2181 0-6-0PT
2184	2188	2190

Class 2251 0-6-0
2209	2259	2297	3206
2232	2262	3203	

Class 1501 0-6-0PT
2716	2719

Class 28xx 2-8-0
2822	2840	2871	2878	3825

Class ROD 2-8-0
3026	3028

Class 43xx 2-6-0
4375	5334	6311	7305
5315	5365	6316	7310
5319	6303	6327	7313

Class 57xx 0-6-0PT
5742	5774	9669

Class 64xx 0-6-0PT
6404	6405	6422

Class 56xx 0-6-2T
6694	6698

Class 74xx 0-6-0PT
7403	7414	7433	7443
7409	7431	7440	7447

'Manor' 4-6-0
7817 Garsington Manor

Total 54

Allocations: 1959 (84J)

Class 16xx 0-6-0PT
1635	1659	1660

Class 28xx 2-8-0
2840	2855	2871	2878	3828

Class 57xx 0-6-0PT
3689	4645	8727	9621	9793
4617	5774	8791	9669	

Class 43xx 2-6-0
6316	6339	7310	7313

Class 64xx 0-6-0PT
6405	6429

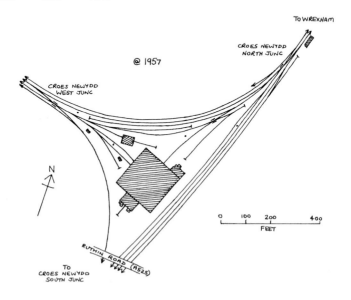

64

Class 56xx 0-6-2T
| 6611 | 6617 | 6632 | 6694 | 6696 |

Class 74xx 0-6-0PT
| 7403 | 7414 | 7431 | 7440 | 7443 |
| 7409 | 7428 | 7433 | 7442 | |

'Manor' 4-6-0
7817 Garsington Manor

Class 90xx 4-4-0
| 9004 | 9014 | 9018 |

Total 41

Allocations: 1965 (6C)

Class 16xx 0-6-0PT
| 1628 | 1638 | 1660 |

Class 57xx 0-6-0PT
| 3749 | 4645 | 9610 | 9639 |
| 3789 | 4683 | 9630 | 9669 |

Class 28xx 2-8-0
| 3813 | 3817 | 3849 | 3850 | 3855 |

Class 56xx 0-6-2T
| 5667 | 6604 | 6625 | 6651 |
| 5676 | 6611 | 6626 | 6665 |

Class 2MT 2-6-2T
| 41204 | 41241 |

Class 8F 2-8-0
| 48325 | 48665 |

Class 4MT 4-6-0
| 75009 | 75021 | 75024 | 75029 | 75071 |

Class 4MT 2-6-4T
| 80078 | 80079 | 80080 |

The northern entrance to Croes Newydd shed in April 1964 with the coaling ramp on the right.
I. L. Stevenson

Class 2MT 2-6-2T
| 84000 | 84004 |

Total 38

Croes Newydd (Wrexham) was recognised as 89B from October 1960 although the recoding was not given official status until January 1961.

The shed was further coded 6C when the London Midland Region took control in September 1963.

It closed in June 1967 and the bulk of remaining locos went to Stoke 5D.

Croes Newydd interior in 1964 depicting the over-girder type of turntable within. By this year the depot had become 6C of the London Midland Region and the domination of GWR types was at an end. IAL

84K CHESTER

Pre-Grouping Origin: GWR
Gazetteer Ref: 20 D4
Closed: 1960
Shed-Codes: 84K (1949-1958)
6E (1958-1960)
Allocations: 1950 (84K)

KEY 1 : EX G.W.R. BUILDING.
2 : EX L.N.W.R. BUILDING.

@ 1958

Class 14xx 0-4-2T
1434

Class 2301 0-6-0
2513

Class 28xx 2-8-0

2810	2882	3858	3860
2812	2890	3859	

'Saint' 4-6-0
2915 Saint Bartholomew
2926 Saint Nicholas
2953 Titley Court

Class 57xx 0-6-0PT

3619	3762	5723	9728
3646	3786	5725	9774
3665	4617	5791	9794

'Castle' 4-6-0
4076 Carmarthen Castle
5033 Broughton Castle
5075 Wellington

'Hall' 4-6-0
4905 Barton Hall
4918 Dartington Hall
4976 Warfield Hall
4987 Brockley Hall
5912 Queen's Hall
5923 Colston Hall

5966 Ashford Hall
6941 Fillongley Hall

Class 51xx 2-6-2T

5103	5141	5179	5184
5129	5174	5181	5186

Class 43xx 2-6-0

5331	5399	6337	6380
5344	6308	6339	6392

Class 56xx 0-6-2T

5647	5690	6624

Class WD 2-8-0

90214	90572	90686

Total 57

Allocations: 1959 (6E)

Class 57xx 0-6-0PT

3630	3786	8709	9728
3665	4602	8729	9794
3676	7762	8730	

Class 51xx 2-6-2T
5174

Class 43xx 2-6-0

5399	6345	6380

A northerly view of the ex-LNWR building at Chester in 1955. The shed was abandoned by the LNWR in 1870 upon the opening of larger premises (see 6A — London Midland Volume). The GWR eventually took it over to relieve the chronic shortage of space at its own site close by (see map). W. Potter

Class 3 2-6-2T
40106   40116

'Jubilee' 4-6-0
45613 *Kenya*
45624 *St Helena*
45632 *Tonga*

Class 8F 2-8-0
48303	48408	48417	48430
48344	48412	48418	48444
48402	48415	48424	48471

Class 5 4-6-0
73013	73021	73024	73026	73038
73014	73023	73025	73033	

Class 4 4-6-0
| 75005 | 75006 | 75020 | 75026 | 75028 |

Class 3 2-6-2T
82001	82003	82032	82036
82002	82005	82034	

Class WD 2-8-0
90214   90686

Total 55

Chester GWR, or Chester West as it was sometimes known, became London Midland Region property in February 1958 and adopted the code 6E.

The shed closed in April 1960 and all its remaining locos went to Chester (Midland) 6A.

Looking north to the ex-GWR portion of Chester West in 1950. The coaling stage is on the right and a 'Dean Goods' 0-6-0 (Class 2301) can be seen in the centre of the view. B. Hilton

85A WORCESTER

Pre-Grouping Origin: GWR
Gazetteer Ref: 9 B3
Closed: 1965
Shed-Code: 85A (1949-1965)
Allocations: 1950

Class 14xx 0-4-2T

1408	1418	5815	5816

Class 1901 0-6-0PT

2001	2016

Class 2021 0-6-0PT

2093	2100	2101

Class 2251 0-6-0

2205	2241	2263	2278	3214
2207	2242	2274	2290	3219
2237	2247	2277	2294	

Class 2301 0-6-0

2458	2551

Class 2721 0-6-0PT

2743

Class ROD 2-8-0

3022	3029	3048

'Bulldog' 4-4-0

3377
3447 *Jackdaw*

Class 57xx 0-6-0PT

3607	4613	4629	4664
3725	4614	4641	7750

Class 28xx 2-8-0

3839

'Star' 4-6-0

4007 *Swallowfield Park*
4051 *Princess Helena*

'Castle' 4-6-0

4082 *Windsor Castle*
4086 *Builth Castle*
4092 *Dunraven Castle*
5017 *St Donats Castle*
5063 *Earl Baldwin*
5092 *Tresco Abbey*
7005 *Lamphey Castle*
7007 *Great Western*

Class 51xx 2-6-2T

4114	4139	4140	5173

Class 45xx 2-6-2T

4546	4596	5573

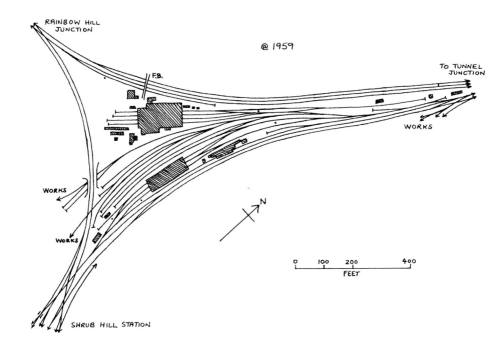

@ 1959

An overhead southerly view of the two buildings at Worcester shed in August 1963. J. L. Stevenson

'Hall' 4-6-0
4993 *Dalton Hall*
5914 *Ripon Hall*
5917 *Westminster Hall*
6930 *Aldersey Hall*
6938 *Corndean Hall*
6947 *Helmingham Hall*
6950 *Kingsthorpe Hall*

Class 43xx 2-6-0

5303	6324	6396
6306	6378	7301

'Grange' 4-6-0
6807 *Birchwood Grange*
6851 *Hurst Grange*
6877 *Llanfair Grange*

Class 72xx 2-8-2T

7222	7236	7240	7248

Class 74xx 0-6-0PT
7437

Class 81xx 2-6-2T
8106

Class WD 2-8-0

90284	90715

Total 81

Allocations: 1959

Class 16xx 0-6-0PT

1629	1661

Class 2251 0-6-0

2206	2243	3205	3214	3217
2209	2247	3213	3216	3218

Class 57xx 0-6-0PT

3605	3775	4625	7707
3607	4613	4629	7777
3725	4614	4664	8737

'Castle' 4-6-0
4088 *Dartmouth Castle*
4089 *Donnington Castle*
5029 *Nunney Castle*
5037 *Monmouth Castle*
5042 *Winchester Castle*
5071 *Spitfire*
5081 *Lockheed-Hudson*
7005 *Sir Edward Elgar*
7007 *Great Western*

Class 51xx 2-6-2T

4109	4124	4152	5179
4113	4142	4154	

'Hall' 4-6-0
4952 *Peplow Hall*
5917 *Westminster Hall*
5952 *Cogan Hall*
5956 *Horsley Hall*
5971 *Merevale Hall*
5980 *Dingley Hall*
5984 *Linden Hall*
5994 *Roydon Hall*
6947 *Helmingham Hall*
6948 *Holbrooke Hall*
6950 *Kingsthorpe Hall*
6984 *Owsden Hall*
7920 *Coney Hall*
7928 *Wolf Hall*

'Grange' 4-6-0
6807 *Birchwood Grange*

69

6820 *Kingstone Grange*
6851 *Hurst Grange*
6856 *Stowe Grange*
6877 *Llanfair Grange*

Class 43xx 2-6-0
7319   7338

Class 81xx 2-6-2T
8106

Class 94xx 0-6-0PT
8427   8496   9429   9466   9486
8480   9401   9455   9480

Class 4 4-6-0
75003   75025

Class 2 2-6-0
78001   78008   78009

Class 3 2-6-2T
82008   82030   82038

Total 79

Allocations: 1965

Class 2251 0-6-0
2222   2244

Class 57xx 0-6-0PT
3615   3682   4664   4680   8793

Class 51xx 2-6-2T
4113   4161

'Hall' 4-6-0
5971 *Merevale Hall*
6958 *Oxburgh Hall*
7904 *Fountains Hall*
7909 *Heveningham Hall*
7919 *Runter Hall*
7920 *Coney Hall*

Class 61xx 2-6-2T
6147   6155   6169

'Grange' 4-6-0
6813 *Eastbury Grange*
6819 *Highnam Grange*
6836 *Estevarney Grange*
6848 *Toddington Grange*
6856 *Stowe Grange*

Class 94xx 0-6-0PT
8415

Total 24

Worcester shed closed in December 1965 and all its locos went for scrap.

Gloucester Horton Road shed in October 1965 as viewed from the end of the coaling ramp. The loco on the left is No 7029 Clun Castle *which was allocated to the shed at the time (now preserved).* W. Potter

85B GLOUCESTER HORTON ROAD

Pre-Grouping Origin: GWR
Gazetteer Ref: 9 E3
Closed: 1965
Shed-Code: 85B (1949-1965)
Allocations: 1950

Class 14xx 0-4-2T

1402	1406	1413	1441	1464
1404	1409	1424	1456	

Class 16xx 0-6-0PT

1612	1616	1623	1625

Class 1901 0-6-0PT

1943	1989	2009

Class 2021 0-6-0PT

2025	2044	2131	2153
2034	2080	2144	2155
2043	2121	2146	

Class 2251 0-6-0

2248	2291	3205
2254	3204	3213

Class 2301 0-6-0

2339	2350

Class 28xx 2-8-0

2823	3848

'Saint' 4-6-0

2938 *Corsham Court*
2951 *Tawstock Court*

Class 3150 2-6-2T

3153	3163	3164	3171

Class 57xx 0-6-0PT

3609	4659	8701	8781
4627	7723	8717	9727
4628	7741	8731	

'Star' 4-6-0

4059 *Princess Patricia*

'Castle' 4-6-0

4079 *Pendennis Castle*
5042 *Winchester Castle*
7006 *Lydford Castle*

Class 51xx 2-6-2T

4141	4174	5112	5114

Class 45xx 2-6-2T

4534	4567	5530	5574
4564	5518	5538	

'Hall' 4-6-0

4929 *Goytrey Hall*
4977 *Watcombe Hall*
4996 *Eden Hall*
5951 *Clyffe Hall*
5980 *Dingley Hall*
5988 *Bostock Hall*
5990 *Durford Hall*
6917 *Oldlands Hall*
6921 *Borwick Hall*
6940 *Didlington Hall*
6987 *Sherrington Hall*
6992 *Arborfield Hall*

Class 43xx 2-6-0

5312	5347	6309	6385
5336	5394	6341	7303
5345	5398	6381	7312

Class 56xx 0-6-2T

6631

'Manor' 4-6-0

7815 *Fritwell Manor*
7818 *Granville Manor*

Class WD 2-8-0

90179	90413	90691

Total 99

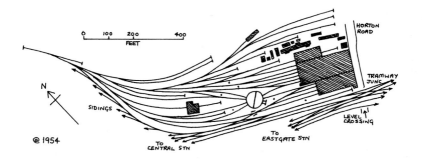

Allocations: 1959

Class 14xx 0-4-2T

1424	1427	1441	1472
1426	1428	1467	

Class 16xx 0-6-0PT

1605	1623	1630	1632	1642
1616	1627	1631	1639	

Class 2251 0-6-0

2207	2248	2253	2291	3203

Class 28xx 2-8-0

2854	3803	3848

Class 57xx 0-6-0PT

3609	4680	7700	7741	8731
4628	5763	7723	8717	8743

'Castle' 4-6-0
4085 Berkeley Castle
5017 The Gloucestershire Regiment 28th, 61st
5094 Tretower Castle

Class 51xx 2-6-2T

4100	4116	4141	5177	5194
4101	4123	4165	5182	5198

Class 43xx 2-6-0

4358	6330	6373	6394
6304	6365	6381	7312

Class 45xx 2-6-2T

4573	5514	5538

'Hall' 4-6-0
4929 Goytrey Hall
5914 Ripon Hall
5951 Clyffe Hall
6917 Oldlands Hall
6985 Parwick Hall
7926 Willey Hall

Class 54xx 0-6-0PT

5417	5418	5421

Class 61xx 2-6-2T
6137

Class 64xx 0-6-0PT
6415

Class 56xx 0-6-2T

6669	6690

'Manor' 4-6-0
7808 Cookham Manor
7809 Childrey Manor
7810 Draycott Manor
7815 Fritwell Manor

Class 94xx 0-6-0PT

8487	9438	9445	9471	9492
8488	9441	9464	9475	

Total 84

Allocations: 1965

Class 2251 0-6-0

2242	2287

Class 57xx 0-6-0PT

3616	3675	3759	4689	8745
3643	3677	3775	4698	

Class 51xx 2-6-2T
4100

'Castle' 4-6-0
5042 Winchester Castle
7022 Hereford Castle
7029 Clun Castle
7034 Ince Castle

'Hall' 4-6-0
5992 Horton Hall
6956 Mottram Hall
6989 Wightwick Hall
6993 Arthog Hall

Class 61xx 2-6-2T
6113

'Manor' 4-6-0
7808 Cookham Manor

Class 94xx 0-6-0PT
9453

Class 4F 0-6-0

44123	44422	44560

Class 5MT 4-6-0

73021	73031	73091

Class 2MT 2-6-0

78001	78004	78006

Class 9F 2-10-0

92000	92007	92238

Total 35

Gloucester Horton Road shed closed in December 1965 and all its locos were withdrawn.

85C HEREFORD

Pre-Grouping Origin: GWR
Gazetteer Ref: 9 C1
Closed: 1964
Shed-Codes: 85C (1949-1960)
86C (1960-1964)
Allocations: 1950 (85C)

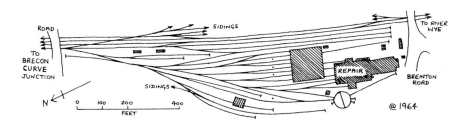

Class AD 2-6-2T
1206

Class 14xx 0-4-2T

1445	1460	5808	5817
1455	5807	5814	

Class 2021 0-6-0PT

2026	2099	2138
2040	2115	2160

Class 2251 0-6-0

2243	2282	2286	3209

Class 2301 0-6-0

2349	2515	2541

Class 28xx 2-8-0
2807

'Saint' 4-6-0
2920 Saint David
2937 Clevedon Court
2944 Highnam Court

'Bulldog' 4-4-0
3406 Calcutta

Class 57xx 0-6-0PT

3728	4600	4678	7707
3789	4657	5765	9619

Class 43xx 2-6-0

5348	6326	6352	7307	7314
5377	6349	6395	7308	

Class 56xx 0-6-2T
6681

'Hall' 4-6-0
6905 Claughton Hall
6916 Misterton Hall
6936 Breccles Hall
6951 Impney Hall
6984 Owsden Hall
6989 Wightwick Hall

Class 74xx 0-6-0PT

7416	7420

Class WD 2-8-0
90524

Total 53

Allocations: 1959 (85C)

Class 14xx 0-4-2T

1445	1455

Class 16xx 0-6-0PT

1617	1625	1657	1662	1667

Class 2251 0-6-0

2241	2242	2249	2266	2295

Class 57xx 0-6-0PT

3728	4659	8722	8787	9717
4657	4678	8781	9665	

Class 51xx 2-6-2T
4115

Class 42xx 2-8-0T

5226	5243	5245

Class 43xx 2-6-0
5350   6359   7326

'Hall' 4-6-0
5998 *Trevor Hall*
6989 *Wightwick Hall*
6992 *Arborfield Hall*

Class 74xx 0-6-0PT
7401   7426   7437

Class 2 2-6-0
78004

Total 35

Hereford shed closed in November 1964 and the majority of its remaining locos went to Gloucester Horton Road 85B, Severn Tunnel Junction 86E and Cardiff Radyr 88B.

Hereford shed and coaler from the north in 1964.
J. L. Stevenson

The rear of Hereford shed in 1963 showing the repair shed on the left of the picture.   K. Fairey

85D KIDDERMINSTER

Origin: GWR (1932)
Gazetteer Ref: 9 A3
Closed: 1964
Shed Codes: 85D (1949-1960)
84G (1960-1963)
2P (1963-1964)
Allocations: 1950 (85D)

Allocations: 1959 (85D)

Class 57xx 0-6-0PT
3601	8701	8718

Class 51xx 2-6-2T
4114	4153	4175	5110

Class 43xx 2-6-0
5333	5355	5396	6314	6382

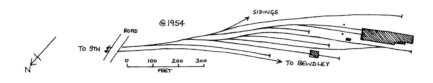

Class CMDP 0-6-0ST + 0-6-0PT*
29	29*

Class 2021 0-6-0PT
2051

Class 57xx 0-6-0PT
3601	4625	7700	8718	8727

Class 51xx 2-6-2T
4100	4153	4175	5110

Class 45xx 2-6-2T
4578	4584	4586	4594	4599

Class 43xx 2-6-0
6382

Class 81xx 2-6-2T
8101

Total 19

Class 45xx 2-6-2T
5518

Class 56xx 0-6-2T
6679

Class 81xx 2-6-2T
8101

Total 15

Kidderminster became 84G in October 1960 and latterly 2P when the London Midland Region took control in September 1963.

The depot closed in August 1964 and the remaining locos transferred to Stourbridge 2C (ex-84F).

Class 3 2-6-2T No 82008 (84E) stands outside Kidderminster shed in June 1953.   B. Hilton

86A EBBW JUNCTION

Pre-Grouping Origin: GWR
Gazetteer Ref: 43 A4
Closed: 1965
Shed-Codes: 86A (1949-1963)
86B (1963-1965)
Allocations: 1950 (86A)

@ 1955

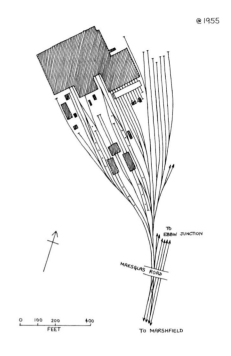

Class BM 0-6-2T
431   432   435   436

Class 15xx 0-6-0PT
1509

Class 1854 0-6-0PT
1862

Class 2021 0-6-0PT
2063   2073   2122

Class 2251 0-6-0
2218   2227   2239   2280

Class 28xx 2-8-0

2815	2842	2876	3800	3810
2817	2851	2879	3801	3816
2819	2861	2889	3804	3830
2821	2865	2894	3805	3833
2834	2866	2896	3807	3836

'Saint' 4-6-0
2936 *Cefntilla Court*
2979 *Quentin Durward*

Class 31xx 2-6-2T
3103

Class 57xx 0-6-0PT

3634	3714	5732	7781	9637
3636	3726	5741	8710	9644
3647	3796	7736	8711	9662
3662	3798	7753	8778	9664
3700	4671	7768	9616	9667
3712	5709	7771	9632	9731

Class 51xx 2-6-2T
4137   4148   4156   4168

Class 42xx 2-8-0T

4203	4248	5206	5224	5251
4206	4263	5208	5229	5255
4225	4268	5212	5233	5256
4230	4289	5217	5234	5259
4242	4294	5218	5238	5264
4247	5201	5222	5243	

'Hall' 4-6-0
4941 *Llangedwyn Hall*
5906 *Lawton Hall*
5911 *Preston Hall*
6927 *Lilford Hall*

Class 43xx 2-6-0
5364

Class 45xx 2-6-2T
5545   5550

Class 56xx 0-6-2T
5602   6654   6672

Class 64xx 0-6-0PT
6409   6415   6426   6428   6439

'Grange' 4-6-0
6820 *Kingstone Grange*
6821 *Leaton Grange*
6834 *Dummer Grange*
6870 *Bodicote Grange*
6874 *Haughton Grange*

Class 72xx 2-8-2T

7203	7217	7245	7252
7214	7231	7247	7253
7215	7241	7249	

Class 94xx 0-6-0PT
8406   8450   8453

Class WD 2-8-0
90167   90261   90565

Total 141

Allocations: 1959 (86A)

Class 15xx 0-6-0PT
1509

Class 16xx 0-6-0PT
1653   1656

Class 2251 0-6-0
2218   2227

Class 28xx 2-8-0

2839	2868	3804	3808	3833
2842	2894	3805	3827	3853
2845	2898	3806	3830	
2858	3800	3807	3832	

Class 31xx 2-6-2T
3103

Class 57xx 0-6-0PT

3634	3772	7755	8710	9664
3636	3798	7768	8711	9667
3662	4611	7771	8766	9674
3691	4671	7774	9616	9745
3712	5709	7781	9644	9746
3714	7736	7787	9662	

Class 42xx 2-8-0T

4203	4247	4290	5228	5251
4211	4248	5201	5229	5255
4227	4267	5205	5233	5256
4229	4283	5217	5234	5259
4246	4286	5227	5238	

'Hall' 4-6-0
4916 Crumlin Hall

Class 51xx 2-6-2T
5173   5188

Class 56xx 0-6-2T
5657

Class 43xx 2-6-0
6348   6370

Class 64xx 0-6-0PT
6412   6417   6425   6426

'Grange' 4-6-0
6838 Goodmoor Grange
6847 Tidmarsh Grange
6865 Hopton Grange

Class 72xx 2-8-2T

7212	7222	7233	7243	7253
7218	7229	7234	7245	
7219	7231	7240	7250	

Class 94xx 0-6-0PT

8440	8493	8499	9468	9490
8453	8495	9427	9482	

Class WD 2-8-0

90069	90149	90225	90544	90676

Class 9F 2-10-0

92000	92002	92006	92242	92248
92001	92004	92007	92243	92249

Total 127

Allocations: 1965 (86B)

Class 57xx 0-6-0PT

3662	3767	4260	9649	9666
3708	3772	9600	9662	

Class 28xx 2-8-0

3808	3837	3861
3830	3840	3864

Class 42xx 2-8-0T

4253	4268	5209	5235	5241

'Hall' 4-6-0
5961 Toynbee Hall
6978 Haroldstone Hall

Class 9F 2-10-0

92225	92226	92230	92235	92237

Total 27

Ebbw Junction became 86B in September 1963 and closed in October 1965. The remaining locos went to four other depots: Worcester 85A, Gloucester 85B, Bristol Barrow Road 82E and Oxford 81F.

Looking north across Ebbw Junction shed yard to the large repair shed at the depot in 1955.   N. E. Preedy

86B NEWPORT PILL

Pre-Grouping Origin: Alexandra Docks Rly
Gazetteer Ref: 43 A3
Closed: 1963
Shed-Code: 86B (1949-1963)

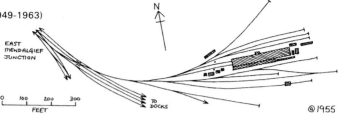

@1955

Allocations: 1950

Class AD 0-6-0T
666	667

Class 15xx 0-6-0PT
1506	1507

Class 1854 0-6-0PT
1709

Class 2021 0-6-0PT
2033	2136	2154

Class 57xx 0-6-0PT
3663	6710	6729	6755	7712
4662	6711	6730	6756	7774
5714	6725	6731	6757	7789
5740	6726	6732	6759	8796
5747	6727	6735	6760	
5750	6728	6743	6764	

Class 42xx 2-8-0T
4201	4233	4253	4291	5244
4211	4235	4258	5200	5250
4226	4237	4269	5231	5252
4229	4246	4280	5235	5260

Class 56xx 0-6-2T
5638

Total 57

Allocations: 1959

Class 15xx 0-6-0PT
1506	1507

Class 57xx 0-6-0PT
3652	5740	6724	6743	6757
3663	5747	6725	6745	6759
3674	5758	6728	6750	6760
4643	5768	6729	6751	6764
4682	5707	6739	6755	6772
5734	5711	6742	6756	7703

Class 42xx 2-8-0T
4201	4238	4276	5231	5252
4214	4253	4280	5235	5257
4233	4258	5200	5244	
4235	4259	5202	5250	

Total 50

Newport Pill closed in June 1963 and all the remaining engines went to Ebbw Junction 86A.

A host of Newport Pill's '57xx' allocation at rest alongside the south wall of the depot in 1958. Note the huge transporter bridge in the background.
K. Fairey

86C CARDIFF CANTON

Pre-Grouping Origin: GWR
Gazetteer Ref: 43 B4
Closed: 1962
Shed-Codes: 86C (1949-1960)
88A (1960-1962)
Allocations: 1950 (86C)

Class TV 0-6-2T

203	208	220	357
205	209	335	381

Class BM 0-6-2T
425

Class 2301 0-6-0

2407	2537

Class 28xx 2-8-0

2820	2877	3809	3814	3823
2837	2891	3812	3817	3824

'Saint' 4-6-0
2906 *Lady of Lynn*
2940 *Dorney Court*
2943 *Hampton Court*

Class ROD 2-8-0
3036

Class 57xx 0-6-0PT

3670	4633	5786	9648
3729	4677	8723	9713
3755	5749	8728	9723
4622	5776	9629	9759

'Castle' 4-6-0
4083 *Abbotsbury Castle*
4094 *Dynevor Castle*
5001 *Llandovery Castle*
5005 *Manorbier Castle*
5006 *Tregenna Castle*
5007 *Rougemont Castle*
5020 *Trematon Castle*
5030 *Shirburn Castle*
5046 *Earl Cawdor*
5049 *Earl of Plymouth*
5052 *Earl of Radnor*
5054 *Earl of Ducie*
5080 *Defiant*
5089 *Westminster Abbey*
5099 *Compton Castle*
7016 *Chester Castle*
7017 *G. J. Churchward*
7020 *Gloucester Castle*
7022 *Hereford Castle*
7023 *Penrice Castle*

Class 51xx 2-6-2T
4145

Class 42xx 2-8-0T

4222	4231	4270	4287
4224	4255	4275	5226
4227	4266	4285	5249

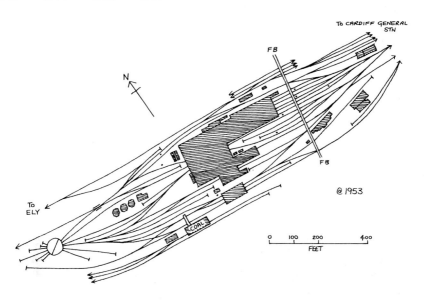

'Hall' 4-6-0
4901 Adderley Hall
4913 Baglan Hall
4952 Peplow Hall
4953 Pitchford Hall
4974 Talgarth Hall
4975 Umberslade Hall
4979 Wootton Hall
5910 Park Hall
5946 Marwell Hall
5953 Dunley Hall
5958 Knolton Hall
5970 Hengrave Hall
5977 Beckford Hall
6928 Underley Hall
6939 Calveley Hall
6943 Farnley Hall
6946 Heatherden Hall
6948 Holbrooke Hall
6969 Wraysbury Hall
6998 Burton Agnes Hall
6999 Capel Dewi Hall

Class 43xx 2-6-0

5307	5382	5388	6353

Class 56xx 0-6-2T

5679	5685

Class 72xx 2-8-2T

7201	7219

Class 94xx 0-6-0PT
8401

Class WD 2-8-0
90271

Total 105

Allocations: 1959 (86C)

Class 15xx 0-6-0PT
1508

Looking north-west to the six lane straight shed at Canton in 1953. The footbridge across connected the carriage sheds which stood either side of the depot. W. Potter

Class 28xx 2-8-0

2834	2889	3809	3835	3855
2864	2891	3810	3842	3860
2874	2895	3816	3843	
2877	3801	3817	3845	

Class 57xx 0-6-0PT

3670	5727	8723	9648	9778
3755	5749	8728	9713	
4622	5776	8776	9723	
4633	7775	9603	9759	

'Castle' 4-6-0
4073 Caerphilly Castle
5095 Barbury Castle
5099 Compton Castle
7023 Penrice Castle

Class 42xx 2-8-0T

4207	4254	4271	5218
4225	4266	4297	5260
4231	4270	5207	5261

'Hall' 4-6-0
4946 Moseley Hall
4956 Plowden Hall
4973 Sweeney Hall
4999 Gopsal Hall
5910 Park Hall
5911 Preston Hall
5946 Marwell Hall
5962 Wantage Hall
5970 Hengrave Hall
6901 Arley Hall
6932 Burwarton Hall
6935 Browsholme Hall
6936 Breccles Hall

6939 *Calveley Hall*
6943 *Farnley Hall*
6958 *Oxburgh Hall*
6963 *Throwley Hall*
6999 *Capel Dewi Hall*
7913 *Little Wyrley Hall*

Class 56xx 0-6-2T
5602   5685   6600

Class 43xx 2-6-0
6308   6326   6333   6352   7332

Class 72xx 2-8-2T
7227

'Manor' 4-6-0
7805 *Broome Manor*

Class 94xx 0-6-0PT
8439   8457   8484   9443   9477
8441   8464   9426   9453   9493
8447   8466   9437   9461   9494

'Britannia' 4-6-2
70016 *Ariel*
70018 *Flying Dutchman*
70019 *Lightning*
70020 *Mercury*
70022 *Tornado*
70023 *Venus*
70024 *Vulcan*
70025 *Western Star*
70026 *Polar Star*
70027 *Rising Star*
70028 *Royal Star*
70029 *Shooting Star*

Class WD 2-8-0

90125	90238	90524	90573	90691
90188	90312	90565	90579	90693
90201	90323	90572	90685	

Class 9F 2-10-0

92003	92231	92233	92235	92237
92005	92232	92234	92236	

Total 131

Canton became 88A in October 1960 and closed in September 1962 when all its locos transferred to Cardiff East Dock 88L (ex-88B). The latter depot reopened to steam power in this month using the entire Canton allocation (see Cardiff East Dock 1962 allocation).

The westerly approaches to Cardiff Canton's roundhouse in July 1952. W. Potter

86D LLANTRISANT

Pre-Grouping Origin: GWR
Gazetteer Ref: 43 C4
Closed: 1964
Shed-Codes: 86D (1949-1960)
88G (1960-1964)
Allocations: 1950 (86D)

Class AD 2-6-2T
1205

Class 14xx 0-4-2T
1421   1471

Class 57xx 0-6-0PT

3612	3656	4620	5788	9780
3617	3691	4674	8739	
3644	3703	5708	9746	

Class 42xx 2-8-0T

| 4208 | 4261 | 5241 |

Total 19

Allocations: 1959 (86D)

Class 57xx 0-6-0PT

3612	3656	4637	5708
3617	3680	4662	5788
3644	4620	4674	9780

Class 42xx 2-8-0T

| 4208 | 4252 | 4268 | 4273 |

Total 16

Llantrisant shed became 88G in October 1960 and closed in October 1964. The remaining engines went to Cardiff Radyr 88B and Cardiff East Dock 88A.

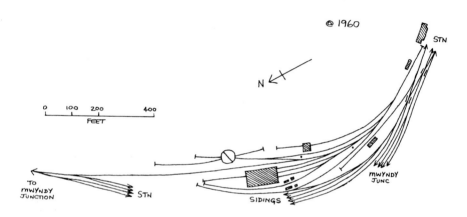

Llantrisant shed in April 1953.   B. K. B. Green

86E SEVERN TUNNEL JUNCTION

Pre-Grouping Origin: GWR
Gazetteer Ref: 8 B2
Closed: 1965
Shed-Code: 86E (1949-1965)
Allocations: 1950

Class 15xx 0-6-0PT
1508

Class 2301 0-6-0
2414   2460

Class 28xx 2-8-0

2804	2887	3808	3838	3850
2829	2892	3815	3843	
2838	3806	3818	3844	

'Saint' 4-6-0
2952 *Twineham Court*

Class 3150 2-6-2T

3150	3161	3170	3176	3185
3154	3167	3172	3177	3188
3157	3168	3174	3183	3190

Class 51xx 2-6-2T
4119   4144

Class 42xx 2-8-0T

4200	4277	4286	5214	5253
4243	4282	5205	5228	5262

Class 43xx 2-6-0
5362   6386

Class 56xx 0-6-2T

5620	5626	6639	6673	6689
5625	5645	6666	6676	

Class 57xx 0-6-0PT

5706	5729	7764	8799	9745

'Grange' 4-6-0
6871 *Bourton Grange*

Class 72xx 2-8-2T

7210	7223	7230	7246
7212	7224	7232	7251
7216	7229	7239	

Class WD 2-8-0
90201   90355   90716

Total 75

Allocations: 1959

Class 2251 0-6-0
2231   2292

Class 28xx 2-8-0

2806	2838	2867	2887	3838
2815	2847	2869	2892	3844
2826	2860	2872	2893	3847
2832	2861	2873	2896	3852
2837	2862	2883	3812	3866

Class 51xx 2-6-2T

4119	4137	4164	5169
4127	4151	5155	5181
4130	4156	5166	5191

Class 42xx 2-8-0T

4215	4289	5214	5236
4217	5212	5224	5253

The western end of Severn Tunnel Junction shed in August 1955 with two 'WD' 2-8-0s responsible for most of the smoke. W. Potter

Severn Tunnel shed from the east in September 1952. W. Potter

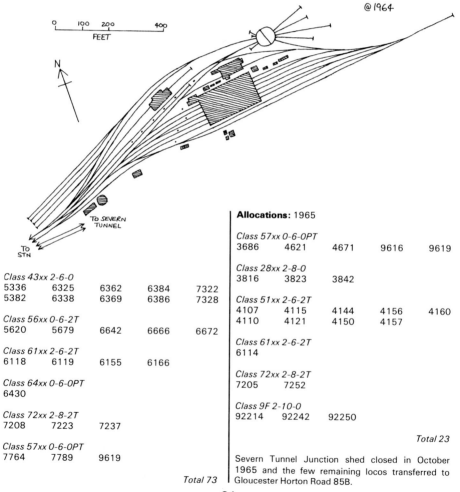

@ 1964

Class 43xx 2-6-0
5336	6325	6362	6384	7322
5382	6338	6369	6386	7328

Class 56xx 0-6-2T
5620	5679	6642	6666	6672

Class 61xx 2-6-2T
6118	6119	6155	6166

Class 64xx 0-6-0PT
6430

Class 72xx 2-8-2T
7208	7223	7237

Class 57xx 0-6-0PT
7764	7789	9619

Total 73

Allocations: 1965

Class 57xx 0-6-0PT
3686	4621	4671	9616	9619

Class 28xx 2-8-0
3816	3823	3842

Class 51xx 2-6-2T
4107	4115	4144	4156	4160
4110	4121	4150	4157	

Class 61xx 2-6-2T
6114

Class 72xx 2-8-2T
7205	7252

Class 9F 2-10-0
92214	92242	92250

Total 23

Severn Tunnel Junction shed closed in October 1965 and the few remaining locos transferred to Gloucester Horton Road 85B.

84

86F TONDU

Pre-Grouping Origin: GWR
Gazetteer Ref: 43 D4
Closed: 1964
Shed-Codes: 86F (1949-1960)
88H (1960-1964)
Allocations: 1950 (86F)

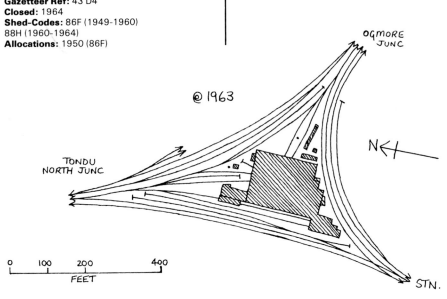

@ 1963

OGMORE JUNC

TONDU NORTH JUNC

N

STN.

0 100 200 400
FEET

Class 1854 0-6-0PT				
1870				

Class 31xx 2-6-2T				
3100				

Class 57xx 0-6-0PT				
3616	3699	5707	7770	8777
3627	3772	5756	7798	9649
3652	4634	5797	8712	9660
3668	4643	7725	8721	9674
3674	4669	7746	8740	9681
3695	4675	7752	8748	

Class 42xx 2-8-0T			
4218	4241	4260	4276
4236	4251	4273	5202

Class 44xx 2-6-2T	
4404	4408

Class 45xx 2-6-2T	
4557	5556

Class 56xx 0-6-2T				
5633	6621	6642	6649	6675

Total 48

Allocations: 1959 (86F)

Class 57xx 0-6-0PT				
3616	4675	7752	8712	9649
3627	5706	7753	8721	9660
3668	7725	7770	8740	
3690	7732	7778	8748	
4669	7746	7798	9609	

Class 51xx 2-6-2T	
4121	4144

Class 42xx 2-8-0T			
4218	4241	4263	4298
4222	4243	4269	5208
4236	4251	4274	

Class 45xx 2-6-2T		
5534	5545	5555

Class 56xx 0-6-2T		
5629	6673	6676

Class 94xx 0-6-0PT			
8448	8497	8498	9451

Total 45

Tondu shed became 88H in October 1960 and closed in April 1964. The displaced locos went to 11 other South Wales sheds but Neath 87A and Barry 88C received the most.

The shed yard at Tondu from a northerly viewpoint in 1951. LGRP, courtesy David & Charles

Three of Tondu's allocation, namely Nos 4675, 4406 and 3668 inside the shed in March 1953 during re-roofing operations. Note that the former loco has still to receive its smokebox number and is dependent upon the old buffer beam method for forward identification. C. H. S. Owen

86G PONTYPOOL ROAD

Pre-Grouping Origin: GWR
Gazetteer Ref: 43 A2
Closed: 1965
Shed-Code: 86G (1949-1965)
Allocations: 1950

Class TV 0-6-2T
349   385

Class 14xx 0-4-2T
1422   5818

Class 2021 0-6-0PT
2021   2035   2094   2117

Class 2301 0-6-0
2385

Class 28xx 2-8-0
2800   2811   2864   2893   3838
2801   2813   2884   3822   3862
2802   2862   2888   3826

Class ROD 2-8-0
3012   3023   3040   3044
3018   3038   3042

Class 57xx 0-6-0PT
3628   3730   4668   7724   9650
3651   3779   5728   7740   9797
3690   4611   5768   8716
3692   4639   5792   8755
3717   4642   6742   8788

Class 51xx 2-6-2T
4121   4131   4138
4130   4135   4158

Class 42xx 2-8-0T
4271

Class 43xx 2-6-0
4303   5355   6333   6370

Class 45xx 2-6-2T
4533   4541   4593   5516   5532

'Hall' 4-6-0
4912 *Berrington Hall*
4932 *Hatherton Hall*
4933 *Himley Hall*
5975 *Winslow Hall*

Class 64xx 0-6-0PT
6400   6424   6430
6403   6429   6432

Class 56xx 0-6-2T
6636   6663   6687

Class 72xx 2-8-2T
7206   7233   7234   7235

Class 74xx 0-6-0PT
7426

Class WD 2-8-0
90268   90563

Total 88

@1962

Pontypool Road's south entrance in October 1962.
W. Potter

The northern entrance to Pontypool Road a decade
earlier with the end of the coaling ramp visible on the
right. W. Potter

5948 *Siddington Hall*
6903 *Belmont Hall*
6928 *Underley Hall*
6946 *Heatherden Hall*

Class 43xx 2-6-0

5318	5330	5381	7325
5321	5345	6368	7334

Class 56xx 0-6-2T

5625	5645	6634	6675	6693
5638	5659	6636	6685	

Class 64xx 0-6-0PT

6400	6424

'Grange' 4-6-0

6802 *Bampton Grange*
6812 *Chesford Grange*
6819 *Highnam Grange*
6840 *Hazeley Grange*
6867 *Peterston Grange*
6872 *Crawley Grange*

Class 72xx 2-8-2T

7201	7206	7213	7246
7204	7210	7220	7251

Class 3 2-6-2T

40091	40145

Class WD 2-8-0

90192	90315	90701

Total 88

Pontypool Road shed closed in May 1965 and the
bulk of the remaining engines went to Cardiff East
Dock 88A and Cardiff Radyr 88B.

Allocations: 1959

Class 2251 0-6-0
2296

Class 28xx 2-8-0

2803	2884	3822	3854
2848	3815	3824	3859
2866	3818	3826	

Class 57xx 0-6-0PT

3628	3717	5750	7724	9730
3640	3779	5756	7740	9796
3651	4600	5759	7796	9797
3685	4639	5775	8707	
3703	4642	5789	8716	
3708	4668	7712	9650	

Class 51xx 2-6-2T

4135	5103

Class 42xx 2-8-0T
4230

Class 45xx 2-6-2T

4593	5564

'Hall' 4-6-0
4926 *Fairleigh Hall*
4943 *Marrington Hall*

86H ABERBEEG

Pre-Grouping Origin: GWR
Gazetteer Ref: 43 B2
Closed: 1964
Shed-Codes: 86H (1949-1960)
86F (1960-1964)
Allocations: 1950 (86H)

Class 57xx 0-6-0PT

3640	3716	4685	7703	8776
3680	3776	4686	7721	8794
3683	4637	5733	7775	9796
3708	4652	5777	7778	
3711	4682	5789	8724	

Class 42xx 2-8-0T

4214	4223	4267	5207
4217	4238	4290	5236

Class 45xx 2-6-2T

4514	4522	4597	5520

Class 56xx 0-6-2T
6685

Class 94xx 0-6-0PT
8402

Total 37

Allocations: 1959 (86H)

Class 57xx 0-6-0PT

3647	3747	4652	5794	8778
3683	4627	4685	8705	8786

Class 42xx 2-8-0T

4237	4277	4287	5206
4250	4285	4291	5241

Class 45xx 2-6-2T

5516	5544	5568

Class 56xx 0-6-2T

6621	6629	6644	6653	6663

Class 94xx 0-6-0PT

8429	8437	8494	9459
8436	8489	9458	9460

Total 34

Aberbeeg shed became 86F in October 1960 and closed in December 1964 when its last locos went to Cardiff East Dock 88A and Cardiff Radyr 88B.

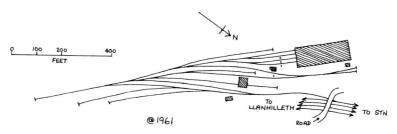

@ 1961

Aberbeeg from an elevated position in 1959 showing the roof detail to good effect. Photomatic

86J ABERDARE

Pre-Grouping Origin: GWR
Gazetteer Ref: 43 D2
Closed: 1965
Shed-Codes: 86J (1949-1960)
88J (1960-1965)
Allocations: 1950 (86J)

Class RR 0-6-2T
65

Class TV 0-6-2T

204	282	284	362	374

Class 2021 0-6-0PT
2159

Class 28xx 2-8-0

2806	2828	2836	2880
2808	2831	2870	

Class 57xx 0-6-0PT

3605	3747	5787	7748	9607
3610	3753	5796	7773	9609
3655	5770	7720	8786	9712

Class 42xx 2-8-0T

4228	4264	5237	5258
4257	4297	5245	5263

Class 56xx 0-6-2T

5649	6622	6651	6692
6605	6628	6652	6693

Class 64xx 0-6-0PT

6410	6413	6437

Class 72xx 2-8-2T

7213	7221	7242

Class 74xx 0-6-0PT
7423

Total 52

Allocations: 1959 (86J)

Class 28xx 2-8-0

2810	2831	2870	3850
2813	2863	2876	

Class 57xx 0-6-0PT

3603	3695	3753	9607
3610	3699	7720	9712
3655	3716	7773	9731

Class 42xx 2-8-0T

4228	4257	4272	5258
4255	4262	5237	5263

Class 56xx 0-6-2T

5624	5698	6628	6661
5633	6605	6651	6687
5649	6622	6652	

Class 43xx 2-6-0
6361

Class 64xx 0-6-0PT

6410	6413	6431	6437

Class 72xx 2-8-2T

7214	7216	7221

Class 74xx 0-6-0PT
7423

Class 94xx 0-6-0PT

8444	8445

Total 49

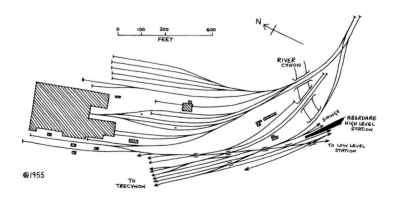

@1955

Aberdare yard and coaler with a pair of '56xx' 0-6-2Ts on the right.   W. Potter

Aberdare shed was re-coded 88J in October 1960 and closed in March 1965. The majority of its remaining locos went to Ebbw Junction 86B, Severn Tunnel Junction 86E and Llanelly 87F.

The interior of Aberdare in 1959 with (left to right) Nos 6605, 4228, 4593 (86G), 6651, 3655 and 5649 (all 86J unless stated).   Photomatic

87A NEATH

Pre-Grouping Origin: GWR
Gazetteer Ref: 43 F3
Closed: 1965
Shed-Code: 87A (1949-1965)
Allocations: 1950

Class RR 0-6-2T
75

Class 1854 0-6-0PT
1855   1858

Class BPGV 0-6-0ST
2192 Ashburnham

Class 2301 0-6-0
2411

Class 2721 0-6-0PT
2722

Class 57xx 0-6-0PT

3611	5703	7742	8715	9756
3621	5720	7743	8775	9779
3741	5746	7757	8782	9783
3757	5778	7767	9627	9786
3766	7701	7769	9666	9792
3774	7737	7786	9734	
4621	7739	7799	9750	

Class 51xx 2-6-2T
4169

Class 42xx 2-8-0T

4221	4259	4279	4293	5239
4232	4272	4284	4295	5242
4252	4274	4288	5225	5254

Class 81xx 2-6-2T
8104

Class 94xx 0-6-0PT
8420

Total 57

Allocations: 1959

Class 16xx 0-6-0PT
1645

Class 57xx 0-6-0PT

3611	4621	7742	8715	9750
3621	4653	7743	8732	9756
3687	5720	7757	8775	9761
3741	5778	7767	8782	9779
3757	7701	7769	8784	9783
3766	7737	7786	9627	9786
3774	7739	7799	9734	9792

Class 51xx 2-6-2T
4169   5102

Class 42xx 2-8-0T

4221	4275	4282	4295	5239
4242	4279	4284	5222	5242
4264	4281	4288	5225	5246

Class 56xx 0-6-2T
6613   6650

Class 81xx 2-6-2T
8104

Class 94xx 0-6-0PT

8442	9446	9452	9478
9430	9448	9473	

Total 63

The approaches to Neath Court Sart's north-westerly roundhouse in 1959 with the coaler left of centre.
M. Hale

Inside Neath in April 1953 with two '42xx' 2-8-0Ts and an '81xx' 2-6-2T. Left to right are Nos 5225, 5239 and 8104 (all 87A). Photomatic

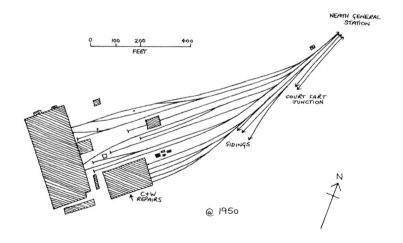

NEATH GENERAL STATION

COURT SART JUNCTION

SIDINGS

C+W REPAIRS

@ 1950

N

0   100   200   400
FEET

Allocations: 1965

Class 57xx 0-6-0PT

3647	3687	4612	9617	9678
3654	3690	4669	9625	9716

Class 56xx 0-6-2T
6628

Total 11

The shed's full title was Neath Court Sart to distinguish it from the two smaller establishments at Glyn Neath (GWR) and Neath (N&BR).

The depot closed in June 1965 and all the locos were withdrawn except Nos 3654 and 4612 which went to Cardiff East Dock 88A.

87B DUFFRYN YARD

Pre-Grouping Origin: Port Talbot Rly
Gazetteer Ref: 43 E3
Closed: 1964
Shed-Code: 87B (1949-1964)
Allocations: 1950

Class RR 0-6-2T

69	70	

Class 16xx 0-6-0PT

1601	1602	1622

Class 2021 0-6-0PT

2079		

Class 57xx 0-6-0PT

3718	5731	6718	7706	9736
3791	5734	6719	7733	9737
4640	5761	6720	7744	9766
4681	5773	6749	9617	9785
4684	6715	6761	9634	9799
5713	6717	6768	9735	

Class 51xx 2-6-2T

4164

Class 42xx 2-8-0T

4212	4265	5216	5257
4256	4292	5220	

Class 56xx 0-6-2T

5612	5646	6629	6686
5629	6616	6644	6691
5639	6623	6650	

Total 54

Allocations: 1959

Class 57xx 0-6-0PT

3613	4681	5787	9617	9742
3718	4684	6701	9634	9766
3762	4695	6761	9735	9785
3791	5738	7706	9736	9799
4640	5770	7758	9737	

Class 42xx 2-8-0T

4256	4292	5216	5254
4265	4293	5220	5264
4278	4296	5221	

Class 56xx 0-6-2T

5604	6602	6620	6686
5688	6616	6623	6691

Class 72xx 2-8-2T

7244	7249

Class 94xx 0-6-0PT

8407	8418	9442	9454	9483
8410	8454	9444	9456	
8416	8490	9447	9457	

Total 58

Duffryn Yard (Port Talbot) shed closed in March 1964 and the majority of the remaining locos went to Neath 87A.

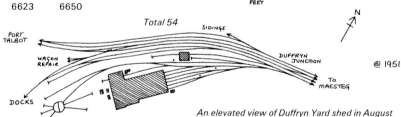

An elevated view of Duffryn Yard shed in August 1948 with most of the locos still bearing GWR insignia. R. S. Carpenter

87C DANYGRAIG

Pre-Grouping Origin: RSB Rly
Gazetteer Ref: 43 F3
Closed: 1960
Shed-Code: 87C (1949-1960)
Allocations: 1950

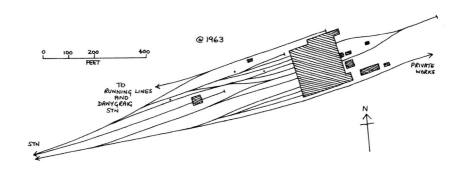

@ 1963

0   100   200   400
FEET

TO
RUNNING LINES
AND
DANYGRAIG
STN

PRIVATE
WORKS

N

STN

Class YTW 0-4-0T
1 Hercules

Class RR 0-6-2T
60

Class LMM 0-6-0T + 0-6-0ST*
359 Hilda*
803

Class 1101 0-4-0T
| 1101 | 1103 | 1105 |
| 1102 | 1104 | 1106 |

Class SHT 0-4-0ST
| 1141 | 1142 | 1143 | 1145 |

Class SHT 0-6-0ST
1147

Class PM 0-4-0ST
| 1151 | 1153 |

Class 16xx 0-6-0PT
1606

Class 2021 0-6-0PT
| 2055 | 2082 | 2134 | 2151 |

Class 57xx 0-6-0PT
| 3781 | 5730 | 6713 | 6762 | 6766 |
| 4694 | 5775 | 6734 | 6763 | 8720 |

Class 42xx 2-8-0T
4299

Total 33

Allocations: 1959

Class 1101 0-4-0T
| 1101 | 1103 | 1105 |
| 1102 | 1104 | 1106 |

Class SHT 0-4-0ST
| 1143 | 1145 |

Class PM 0-4-0ST
1151
Class 16xx 0-6-0PT
| 1634 | 1640 | 1647 | 1648 |

Class 57xx 0-6-0PT
3633	4666	5731	6766	8724
3679	4694	6719	7793	9645
3781	5704	6762	8720	9744

Class 42xx 2-8-0T
4299

Class 74xx 0-6-0PT
7439

Total 30

This ex-Rhondda & Swansea Bay Rly shed began losing its allocation in October 1959 and the bulk of the remaining locos went to Swindon 82C in January 1960. Both portions of the shed continued in use after this date — the running department as diesel only and the repair shop solely for steam.

Looking east to Danygraig shed in June 1953.
B. Hilton

Three of Danygraig's 0-4-0 tank allocation outside the depot in July 1956. Left to right are '1101' class No 1102, 'SHT' class Nos 1142 and 1145. The latter initials stood for Swansea Harbour Trust and scrutiny of the locos' features will show that they were of differing origins. K. Fairey

87D SWANSEA EAST DOCK

Pre-Grouping Origin: GWR
Gazetteer Ref: 43 F3
Closed: 1964
Shed-Code: 87D (1949-1964)
Allocations: 1950

Class TV 0-6-2T
308   309

Class SHT 0-4-0ST
1140   1144

Class SHT 0-6-0ST
1146

Class PM 0-4-0ST
1150   1152

Class BPGV 0-6-0T
2166

Class 57xx 0-6-0PT

3633	5704	7704	9645
3641	5743	7756	9744
3679	6714	9625	

Class 42xx 2-8-0T

4296	5221	5232
5210	5227	5246

Class 56xx 0-6-2T

5616	5628	6613	6662

Class 94xx 0-6-0PT
8408

Total 30

Allocations: 1959

Class SHT 0-4-0ST
1144

Class 16xx 0-6-0PT
1641   1652

Class 57xx 0-6-0PT

3641	7704	7756	9625

Class 42xx 2-8-0T

4232	5211	5240
5210	5232	5262

Class 43xx 2-6-0
5361

Class 56xx 0-6-2T

5616	5628	6662

Class 72xx 2-8-2T

7215	7225	7226	7248

Class 94xx 0-6-0PT

8408	8431	8476	9485
8414	8443	8483	9489
8423	8475	9431	9491

Total 33

Swansea East Dock closed in June 1964 and the remaining engines went to Neath 87A.

Swansea East Dock shed from the coaler in July 1950 with '57xx' 0-6-0PTs dominating the metals.
Real Photos

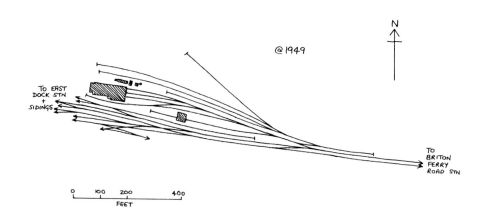

@1949

N

TO EAST
DOCK STN
+
SIDINGS

TO
BRITON
FERRY
ROAD STN

0   100   200   400
            FEET

A visiting '42xx' 2-8-0T No 4297 (86C) facing the
camera at Swansea East Dock in June 1958. Note
the old carriages on the right serving as locker rooms
and stores.   K. Fairey

87E LANDORE

Origin: GWR (1932)
Gazetteer Ref: 43 G3
Closed: 1961
Shed-Code: 87E (1949-1961)
Allocations: 1950

Class 2251 0-6-0
2273

Class 57xx 0-6-0PT

3678	3768	5759	9738	9777
3701	3785	7787	9761	
3713	3797	8789	9775	

'Star' 4-6-0
4003 *Lode Star*
4023
4039 *Queen Matilda*
4048
4050

'Castle' 4-6-0
4074 *Caldicot Castle*
4078 *Pembroke Castle*
4095 *Harlech Castle*
5002 *Ludlow Castle*
5013 *Abergavenny Castle*
5016 *Montgomery Castle*
5051 *Earl Bathurst*
5072 *Hurricane*
5093 *Upton Castle*
7002 *Devizes Castle*

7003 *Elmley Castle*
7009 *Athelney Castle*
7012 *Barry Castle*
7018 *Drysllwyn Castle*
7028 *Cadbury Castle*

Class 51xx 2-6-2T
4134   5162

Class 42xx 2-8-0T

4207	4250	5211	5219

Class 43xx 2-6-0
5341

Class 54xx 0-6-0PT
5400   5408

Class 56xx 0-6-2T

5604	5656	6679	6695
5631	6604	6680	

'Hall' 4-6-0
5913 *Rushton Hall*
5929 *Hanham Hall*
6903 *Belmont Hall*
6918 *Sandon Hall*

Class 64xx 0-6-0PT

6412	6425	6431

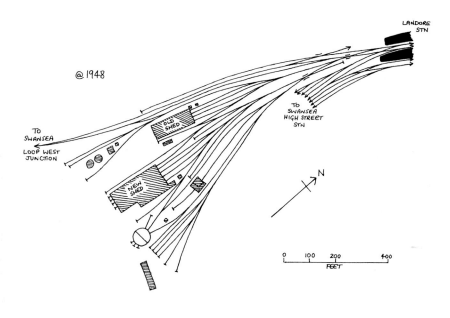

99

An overall view of Landore on a rainy day in 1952.
The 'old shed' is on the right and the 'new' can be
seen in the left background.   W. Potter

Class 72xx 2-8-2T
7211   7225   7244

                                    Total 60

Allocations: 1959

Class 2251 0-6-0
2226   2284

Class 28xx 2-8-0
2821   2844   3849

Class 57xx 0-6-0PT
3678   3768   8788   9637   9775
3701   3785   8789   9715   9777
3713   3797   8794   9738

'Castle' 4-6-0
4074 Caldicot Castle
4076 Carmarthen Castle
4093 Dunster Castle
4094 Dynevor Castle
4097 Kenilworth Castle
4099 Kilgerran Castle
5004 Llanstephen Castle
5013 Abergavenny Castle
5016 Montgomery Castle
5039 Rhuddlan Castle
5041 Tiverton Castle
5051 Earl Bathurst
5077 Fairey Battle
5091 Cleeve Abbey
7002 Devizes Castle
7009 Athelney Castle
7012 Barry Castle

7016 Chester Castle
7028 Cadbury Castle
7035 Ogmore Castle

Class 51xx 2-6-2T
4106   4107

'Hall' 4-6-0
4910 Blaisdon Hall
4923 Evenley Hall
4937 Lanelay Hall
5913 Rushton Hall
5955 Garth Hall
5988 Bostock Hall
5990 Dorford Hall
6905 Claughton Hall
6912 Helmster Hall
6918 Sandon Hall

Class 56xx 0-6-2T
5631   5673   6680   6695
5656   6649   6688

Class 72xx 2-8-2T
7200   7209   7224   7236
7207   7217   7230

Class 94xx 0-6-0PT
8463   9436   9484

                                    Total 68

Landore closed in June 1961 and the remaining
locos were transferred to Neath 87A, Swansea East
Dock 87D and Llanelly 87F.

87F LLANELLY

Origin: GWR (1925)
Gazetteer Ref: 7 B3
Closed: 1965
Shed-Code: 87F (1949-1965)
Allocations: 1950

Class 16xx 0-6-0PT
1607	1609	1614	1618

Class 1901 0-6-0T
1941	1967	2002
1957	1991	2012

Class 2021 0-6-0PT
2027	2081	2085	2126
2042	2083	2098	2150

Class BPGV 0-6-0T + 0-6-0ST*
2162	2165	2167	2168	2176*
2193 Burry Port*				
2196 Gwendraeth*				
2197 Pioneer				
2198				

Class 28xx 2-8-0
2803	2850	2872	3851
2824	2855	3811	

Class 57xx 0-6-0PT
3642	3771	7745	8708	9787
3661	3777	7755	8732	9788
3698	5702	7765	8738	
3719	5705	7776	8749	
3752	5722	7785	8785	
3761	5782	8706	9743	

Class 42xx 2-8-0T
4213	4283	5213	5240
4254	5203	5215	5247
4278	5204	5223	5248
4281	5209	5230	5261

Class 43xx 2-6-0
5335	5378

Class 56xx 0-6-2T
5675	6688

'Hall' 4-6-0
5955 Garth Hall

'Grange' 4-6-0
6810 Blakemere Grange
6824 Ashley Grange

Class 72xx 2-8-2T
7204	7228

Class WD 2-8-0
90315

Total 86

Allocations: 1959

Class 16xx 0-6-0PT
1607	1614	1633	1651	1666
1609	1615	1638	1654	
1612	1622	1643	1655	
1613	1628	1644	1665	

Class 28xx 2-8-0
2808	2824	3811	3851

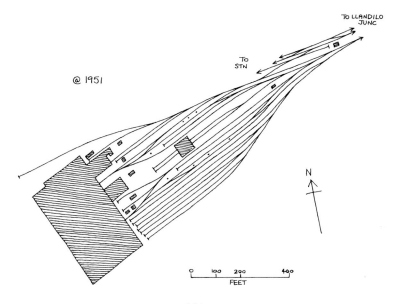

@ 1951

To LLANDILO JUNC

To STN

N

0   100   200   400
FEET

101

Class 57xx 0-6-0PT

3642	3771	7745	8736	9788
3661	3777	7765	8749	
3719	5702	7776	8785	
3752	5705	7785	9652	
3761	7718	8708	9743	

Class 42xx 2-8-0T

4213	5203	5213	5223	5248
4223	5204	5215	5230	5249
4260	5209	5219	5247	

'Hall' 4-6-0
4941 *Llangedwyn Hall*
5902 *Howick Hall*
5909 *Newton Hall*
5953 *Dunley Hall*
5961 *Toynbee Hall*

Class 43xx 2-6-0

5332	6310	7314	7321
5341	7307	7320	

Class 56xx 0-6-2T
5612

'Grange' 4-6-0
6810 *Blakemere Grange*
6818 *Hardwick Grange*
6843 *Poulton Grange*
6844 *Penhydd Grange*

Class 72xx 2-8-2T

7203	7211	7228	7232	7235

Class 94xx 0-6-0PT

8467	8474	8477	9465

Total 82

Allocations: 1965

Class 16xx 0-6-0PT

1607	1623	1651
1611	1643	1669

Class 57xx 0-6-0PT

3671	4668	4676	9631
4604	4675	9609	

Class 56xx 0-6-2T

6613	6643	6691

Class 72xx 2-8-2T

7232	7248	7249

Class 8F 2-8-0

48706	48732	48760

Total 22

The ex-Burry Port & Gwendraeth shed at Burry Port was a sub-shed to Llanelly as the presence of the ex-BPGV locos amongst the 1950 list suggests. The sole survivor of the class became 2198 and was withdrawn from Llanelly in March 1959.

Llanelly shed closed in November 1965 and the few remaining engines went for scrapping.

An interior view of Llanelly in June 1951 showing the boarded turntable. Compare this with those depicted in the Ebbw Junction and Swindon interiors. B. Hilton

87G CARMARTHEN

Pre-Grouping Origin: GWR
Gazetteer Ref: 13 G4
Closed: 1964
Shed-Code: 87G (1949-1964)
Allocations: 1950

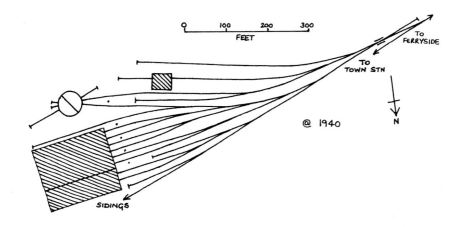

Class 14xx 0-4-2T
1472   5819

Class 16xx 0-6-0PT
1613

Class 1901 0-6-0PT
1903

Class 2021 0-6-0PT
2056   2069   2111

Class 2251 0-6-0
2216   2236   2272
2217   2271   2284

Class 2301 0-6-0
2431   2474

Class ROD 2-8-0
3010   3011   3015

Class 51xx 2-6-2T
4178

'Hall' 4-6-0
4910 Blaisdon Hall
4915 Condover Hall
4922 Enville Hall
4937 Lanelay Hall
4981 Abberley Hall
4984 Albrighton Hall

5963 Wimpole Hall
5972 Olton Hall
5984 Linden Hall
6919 Tylney Hall

Class 43xx 2-6-0
5339   6310   6344
6304   6331   6367

'Grange' 4-6-0
6818 Hardwick Grange

'Castle' 4-6-0
7021 Haverfordwest Castle

Class 74xx 0-6-0PT
7400   7407   7425
7401   7419   7444

Total 43

Allocations: 1959

Class 2251 0-6-0
2216   2224   2272   2274   2290

Class 51xx 2-6-2T
4134

'Hall' 4-6-0
4935 Ketley Hall
4958 Priory Hall

103

4983 *Albert Hall*
5937 *Stanford Hall*
5938 *Stanley Hall*

'Castle' 4-6-0
5006 *Tregenna Castle*
5030 *Shirburn Castle*
5067 *St Fagans Castle*
5080 *Defiant*
7021 *Haverfordwest Castle*

Class 43xx 2-6-0

5353	6305	6329	6377	6393

Class 74xx 0-6-0PT

7400	7407	7422	7444
7402	7419	7425	

'Manor' 4-6-0
7804 *Baydon Manor*
7824 *Iford Manor*
7825 *Lechlade Manor*
7826 *Longworth Manor*
7829 *Ramsbury Manor*

Class 81xx 2-6-2T

8102	8103

Class 57xx 0-6-0PT

8777	9606	9787

Class WD 2-8-0

90167	90179	90207	90485	90529

Total 43

Carmarthen shed closed in April 1964 and the remaining engines were transferred to Llanelly 87F.

Carmarthen depot in 1954. The repair shed forms the taller left-hand building. Photomatic

This June 1958 view of Carmarthen depicts (left to right) '43xx' 2-6-0 No 5310, '2251' 0-6-0 No 2224 (both 87G) and a visiting 'Castle' 4-6-0 No 5077 Fairey Battle (87E). K. Fairey

87H (i) NEYLAND

Pre-Grouping Origin: GWR
Gazetteer Ref: 7 D2
Closed: 1963
Shed-Code: 87H (1949-1963)
Allocations: 1950

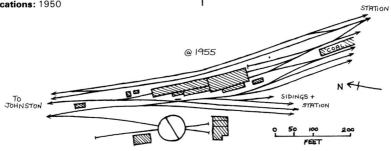

'County' 4-6-0
1001 *County of Bucks*
1009 *County of Carmarthen*
1020 *County of Monmouth*

Class 16xx 0-6-0PT
1611

Class 1901 0-6-0PT
1964   1996   2010   2011

Class 2251 0-6-0
2288

Class 57xx 0-6-0PT
3654   4654   9652

Class 51xx 2-6-2T
4132

Class 43xx 2-6-0
4358	5357	5392	6371
5310	5368	6347	6389
5353	5372	6355	7306

Class 45xx 2-6-2T
4506	4519	4556	4579	5549
4515	4553	4576	5513	5568

'Hall' 4-6-0
4908 *Broome Hall*
4957 *Postlip Hall*
4982 *Acton Hall*
4997 *Elton Hall*

Class 56xx 0-6-2T
5661   6602

Class 74xx 0-6-0PT
7413

'Manor' 4-6-0
7816 *Frilsham Manor*

Class 81xx 2-6-2T
8102   8107

Total 45

Allocations: 1959

'County' 4-6-0
1001 *County of Bucks*
1020 *County of Monmouth*
1027 *County of Stafford*
1029 *County of Worcester*

Class 16xx 0-6-0PT
1601   1611   1637

Class 2251 0-6-0
2208	2228	2251	2273	2288
2220	2229	2259	2283	

Class 57xx 0-6-0PT
3639	4654	5748	8739
3654	4699	8738	9714

Class 51xx 2-6-2T
4122   4132   5180

Class 45xx 2-6-2T
4550	4557	4594	5527	5550
4556	4558	5520	5549	5560

Class 43xx 2-6-0
5357	6389	7318
6306	7306	7340

'Hall' 4-6-0
5903 *Keele Hall*

Class 61xx 2-6-2T
6105

Class 81xx 2-6-2T
8107

Total 46

Neyland shed in June 1958. K. Fairey

Neyland shed closed in September 1963 and most of the remaining engines transferred to the new 87H at Whitland (previously a sub-shed to Neyland).

This GWR view of Neyland in 1947 shows the shed in need of refurbishment and the ash threatening to take over. LGRP, courtesy David & Charles

87H (ii) WHITLAND

Pre-Grouping Origin: GWR
Gazetteer Ref: 7 A1
Closed: 1963
Shed-Code: 87H (1963)
Allocations: November 1963

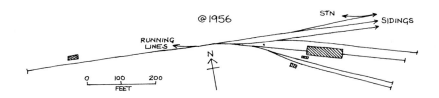

Class 16xx 0-6-0PT
1613

Class 2251 0-6-0
2287

Class 57xx 0-6-0PT
| 3654 | 4654 | 8739 |
| 3712 | 4658 | 9748 |

Class 51xx 2-6-2T
4136

Class 45xx 2-6-2T
| 5508 | 5545 | 5571 |

Class 56xx 0-6-2T
5634

'Manor' 4-6-0
7811 *Dunley Manor*
7825 *Lechlade Manor*

Total 15

Previously a sub-shed to Neyland 87H, Whitland became 87H upon closure of the former depot in September 1963.

It had a very short lifetime as a coded steam shed and closed itself in December 1963. The remaining engines were divided between six other depots but the main beneficiary was Swansea East Dock 87D which received three.

The single lane shed at Whitland in April 1954 with '81xx' class 2-6-2T No 8107 (87H) on the coaling road. Photomatic

87J FISHGUARD GOODWICK

Pre-Grouping Origin: GWR
Gazetteer Ref: 13 F1
Closed: 1963
Shed-Code: 87J (1949-1963)
Allocations: 1950

Class 14xx 0-4-2T
1423   1431   1452

Class 57xx 0-6-0PT
3637   7747   9603
5716   9602   9760

Class 43xx 2-6-0
5395

'Hall' 4-6-0
5905 *Knowsley Hall*
5908 *Moreton Hall*
5928 *Haddon Hall*

'Grange' 4-6-0
6823 *Oakley Grange*

Total 14

Allocations: 1959

Class 2251 0-6-0
2223   2278

Class 57xx 0-6-0PT
3637   5713   9602   9677
4677   7747   9666   9760

'Hall' 4-6-0
4981 *Abberley Hall*
5905 *Knowsley Hall*
5908 *Moreton Hall*
5928 *Haddon Hall*
6909 *Frewin Hall*

Class 43xx 2-6-0
6347

Total 16

Goodwick shed closed in September 1963 and the remaining engines transferred to Duffryn Yard 87B, Old Oak Common 81A, Oxford 81F and Pontypool Road 86G. Three locos were kept in store but these had departed by December the same year.

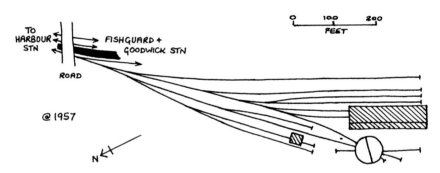

A distant view of Fishguard shed and yard in June 1954.   B. Hilton

88A (i) CARDIFF CATHAYS

Pre-Grouping Origin: Taff Vale Railway
Gazetteer Ref: 43 B4
Closed: 1958 (see notes)
Shed-Code: 88A (1949-1957)
Allocations: 1950

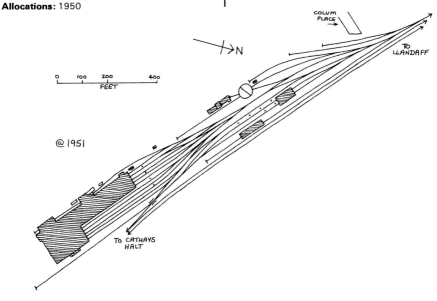

Class RR 0-6-2T

31	38	41	43	56
35	40	42	44	63

Class TV 0-6-2T

286	344	360	377	393
293	345	364	383	
305	346	367	384	
307	347	371	390	
343	348	376	391	

Class BM 0-6-2T

433   434

Class 14xx 0-4-2T

1420   1425   1461

Class 2021 0-6-0PT

2066   2140

Class 57xx 0-6-0PT

3734   4667   7722   7738   8780

Class 54xx 0-6-0PT

5411

Class 56xx 0-6-2T

5601	5672	6607	6634	6665
5623	5678	6608	6635	6682
5636	5681	6612	6647	6684
5640	5687	6618	6659	
5669	5697	6626	6660	
5670	6603	6627	6664	

Class 64xx 0-6-0PT

6402   6423   6435
6416   6433   6436

Class 72xx 2-8-2T

7202   7205

Class 74xx 0-6-0PT

7445

Total 80

Cathays shed lost its code in December 1957 and became a sub-shed to the new 88A at Cardiff Radyr which also received the bulk of Cathays locos. The shed building underwent conversion to DMU maintenance but the yard stayed open for a dozen locos until complete closure in July 1958. The displaced stock was transferred to Radyr 88A and Bristol Bath Road 82A. The final allocation of Cathays was as follows: 3727 5527, 5534, 5568, 6402, 6434, 6635, 6659, 6665, 6682, 82040, 82041 (Total 12).

Cardiff Cathays in 1954 showing the halved covered
accommodation by BR days. The building at the rear
of the open roads served as a repair bay and was
modified from part of the original ten lane structure.
W. Potter

A line of 0-6-2Ts in front of the coaler at Cathays in
1939. The original 10 lane shed can be seen in the
distance.   LGRP, courtesy David & Charles

88A (ii) CARDIFF RADYR

Origin: GWR (1931)
Gazetteer Ref: 43 B4
Closed: 1965
Shed-Codes: 88A (1957-1960)
88B (1960-1965)
Allocations: 1959 (88A)

Class 94xx 0-6-0PT

3401	3405	3409	8460	8478
3402	3406	8420	8469	8481
3403	3407	8438	8470	
3404	3408	8455	8471	

Class 57xx 0-6-0PT

3672	3727	9679

Class 51xx 2-6-2T

4143	4160

Class 56xx 0-6-2T

5640	5692	6618	6647	6684
5648	6603	6624	6648	6689
5663	6606	6626	6659	6699
5669	6607	6633	6660	
5675	6608	6635	6665	
5683	6612	6638	6682	

Class 64xx 0-6-0PT

6411	6434

Class 72xx 2-8-2T

7202	7205	7242

Total 55

Allocations: 1965 (88B)

Class 16xx 0-6-0PT

1612	1655

Class 57xx 0-6-0PT

3644	4650	9615	9656	9682
3717	4662	9622	9667	9780
3784	4679	9644	9675	

Class 51xx 2-6-2T

4132	4169	4177

Class 56xx 0-6-2T

5689	5692	6654	6661	6689
5691	6614	6657	6672	

Class 61xx 2-6-2T

6116

Class 72xx 2-8-2T

7245

Class 94xx 0-6-0PT

8469	8484	9437

Total 33

Radyr was a sub-shed of Cardiff Cathays 88A until December 1957 when the roles were reversed. The shed was recoded 88B in October 1960 and closed in July 1965 when the few remaining locos went to Ebbw Junction 86B and Severn Tunnel Junction 86E.

Cardiff Radyr in October 1960. Locos in front of the shed and facing are (left to right), Nos 6411, 3672, 4160 and 6635 (all Radyr). K. Fairey

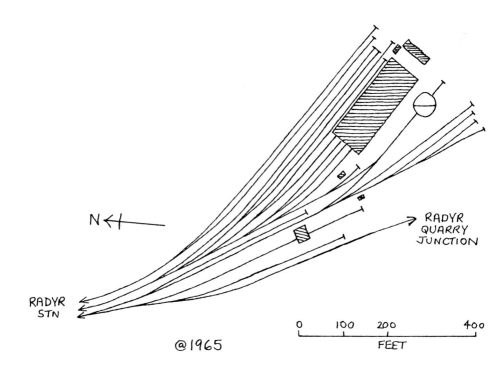

N ←|—

RADYR
QUARRY
JUNCTION

RADYR
STN

@1965

```
0        100     200              400
|——————|——————|——————————————————|
              FEET
```

Radyr shed from the coal stage in 1964 whilst in its final role as 88B, the march of diesels being all too apparent. N. E. Preedy

88B CARDIFF EAST DOCK

Origin: GWR (1931)
Gazetteer Ref: 43 B5
Closed: 1965 (see notes)
Shed-Codes: 88B (1949-1958)
88L (1962-1963)
88A (1963-1965)
Allocations: 1950 (88B)

Class RR 0-6-2T

33	39	67	73
36	55	68	74
37	66	72	

Class RR 0-6-0T

90	92	94	96
91	93	95	

Cardiff Railway 0-6-2T
155

Cardiff Railway 0-6-0ST/PT

681	682	683	684

Class 16xx 0-6-0PT
1610

Class 1854 0-6-0PT
1705

Class 2021 0-6-0PT

2048	2086	2123	2141	2147

Class 2721 0-6-0PT
2754

Class 57xx 0-6-0PT

3672	4630	6704	6721	8743
3681	5710	6705	6744	9677
3707	6700	6706	6751	9679
3783	6701	6707	6765	
4616	6702	6708	6767	
4618	6703	6709	7751	

Class 94xx 0-6-0PT

8414	8416	8455	8457

Total 62

Allocations: September 1962 (88L)

Class 28xx 2-8-0

2887	3804	3810	3862

Class 57xx 0-6-0PT

3755	3784	4633	5749

'Castle' 4-6-0
4080 *Powderham Castle*
5043 *Earl of Mount Edgcumbe*
5073 *Blenheim*
5081 *Lockheed Hudson*
5091 *Cleeve Abbey*
5092 *Tresco Abbey*
5096 *Bridgwater Castle*
5097 *Sarum Castle*
7016 *Chester Castle*

Class 42xx 2-8-0T

4242	5220	5225
4270	5224	5261

'Hall' 4-6-0
4918 *Dartington Hall*
4936 *Kinlet Hall*
4942 *Maindy Hall*
4953 *Pitchford Hall*
5962 *Wantage Hall*
6909 *Frewin Hall*
6912 *Helmster Hall*
6918 *Sandon Hall*
6932 *Burwarton Hall*

Cardiff East Dock MPD in August 1957, seven months before its initial closure. Amongst the locos on shed that day were ex-Rhymney Railway 0-6-2Ts Nos 38 and 42; also ex-Taff Vale Railway 0-6-2Ts Nos 373 and 390. The latter two are visible on the right of the shed buildings. W. Potter

6935 *Browsholme Hall*
6936 *Breccles Hall*
6939 *Calveley Hall*
6944 *Fledborough Hall*
6950 *Kingsthorpe Hall*
6957 *Norcliffe Hall*
6995 *Benthall Hall*
7913 *Little Wyrley Hall*
7925 *Westol Hall*
7927 *Willington Hall*

Class 43xx 2-6-0
6326   6345   7317

Class 56xx 0-6-2T
6681

'Grange' 4-6-0
6822 *Manton Grange*
6847 *Tidmarsh Grange*
6859 *Yiewsley Grange*

'Manor' 4-6-0
7805 *Broome Manor*
7820 *Dinmore Manor*

Class 94xx 0-6-0PT
8445   8471   9426
8466   8484   9461

Class 9F 2-10-0
92003   92216   92236   92244
92208   92219   92237   92246
92210   92232   92241

Total 68

Allocations: 1965 (88A)

Class 57xx 0-6-0PT
3738   4623   4663   9681
3790   4639   9676

Class 42xx 2-8-0T
5202   5208

'Grange' 4-6-0
6815 *Frilford Grange*
6820 *Kingstone Grange*
6837 *Forthampton Grange*
6838 *Goodmoor Grange*
6847 *Tidmarsh Grange*
6859 *Yiewsley Grange*
6869 *Resolven Grange*
6872 *Crawley Grange*
6876 *Kingsland Grange*

'Hall' 4-6-0
6931 *Aldborough Hall*
6944 *Fledborough Hall*
7923 *Speke Hall*
7925 *Westol Hall*
7927 *Willington Hall*

'Manor' 4-6-0
7804 *Baydon Manor*
7811 *Dunley Manor*

Class 9F 2-10-0
92209   92219   92243   92244   92248

Total 30

Cardiff East Dock began losing its allocation in November 1957 and closed in March 1958 when the last few locos went to Barry 88C.

The shed re-opened in September 1962 as 88L with Cardiff Canton's entire redundant stud (see allocation list).

Recoded 88A in September 1963, final closure came in August 1965 with most of the remaining locos transferring to Ebbw Junction 86B and Severn Tunnel Junction 86E.

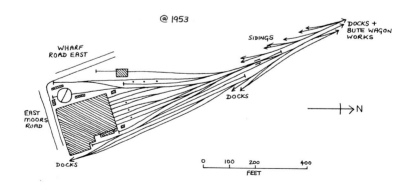

@ 1953

114

88C BARRY

Pre-Grouping Origin: Barry Railway
Gazetteer Ref: 43 C5
Closed: 1964
Shed-Code: 88C (1949-1964)
Allocations: 1950

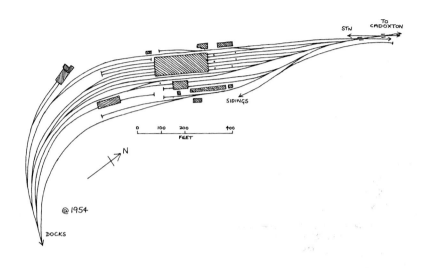

@ 1954

DOCKS

STN
TO CADOXTON
SIDINGS
N
0 100 200 400
FEET

Class RR 0-6-2T

57	58	59

Class BR 0-6-2T

240	267	271	276
263	270	274	

Class TV 0-6-2T

306	361	379	388
312	372	382	389
322	373	387	394

Class 16xx 0-6-0PT

1600	1615

Class 1901 0-6-0PT

1993

Class 51xx 2-6-2T

4160	4161	4163	5183	5195

Class 57xx 0-6-0PT

4601	6723	6740	6750	6769
4690	6724	6745	6752	8735
4692	6733	6746	6753	9631
6712	6736	6747	6754	9676
6722	6738	6748	6758	9776

Class 56xx 0-6-2T

5609	5648	6614	6641	6669
5614	5664	6615	6643	

5621	5665	6619	6653
5627	5667	6620	6658
5632	5699	6637	6668

Class 94xx 0-6-0PT

8451	8458	8460	8461

Total 80

Allocations: 1959

Class 57xx 0-6-0PT

4618	6752	6773	7751
4632	6754	6775	7766
4667	6765	7717	8780

Class 56xx 0-6-2T

5609	5619	5664	6637	6658
5614	5621	5667	6641	
5615	5622	6615	6643	

Class 72xx 2-8-2T

7241	7252

Class 94xx 0-6-0PT

8419	8446	8450	9425

Total 31

Barry shed closed in September 1964 and the majority of its remaining locos transferred to Cardiff Radyr 88B.

The northern end of Barry shed in June 1951, depicting '57xx' 0-6-0PT No 6712 of the depot receiving attention outside. N. E. Preedy

Barry shed from the south in 1958. Photomatic

88D (i) MERTHYR

Pre-Grouping Origin: GWR
Gazetteer Ref: 43 C2
Closed: 1964
Shed-Code: 88D (1949-1964)
Allocations: 1950

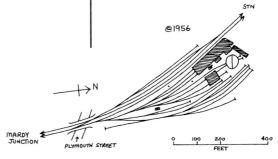

Class RR 0-6-2T

76	78	80	82
77	79	81	83

Class TV 0-6-2T

211	292	370	398
217	316	375	

Class 2721 0-6-0PT

2760

Class 57xx 0-6-0PT

4632	5721	7717	8736	9638
4635	5769	7766	9618	9643
5711	5793	7772	9622	9675

Class 56xx 0-6-2T

5603	5652	5660	5677	5698
5605	5653	5662	5683	
5617	5654	5666	5692	
5622	5655	5671	5694	
5635	5659	5674	5696	

Class 64xx 0-6-0PT

6408	6427	6434

Total 55

Allocations: 1959

Class 57xx 0-6-0PT

3681	9618	9643	9747
4635	9631	9675	9776
4690	9638	9676	

Class 56xx 0-6-2T

5603	5635	5655	5666	5674
5605	5636	5660	5670	5677
5626	5650	5661	5671	5681
5630	5652	5662	5672	5696

Class 64xx 0-6-0PT

6416	6433	6436

Total 34

At closure in November 1964 most of the engines went to the new 88D at Rhymney (see Rhymney 1964 allocation) but a few found homes at Neath 87A, Ebbw Junction 86B and Llanelly 87F.

Ex-Taff Vale 0-6-2T No 217 stands behind '57xx' 0-6-0PT No 9643 (both 88D) in this August 1951 view of Merthyr shed.   W. Potter

88D (ii) RHYMNEY

Pre-Grouping Origin: Rhymney Railway
Gazetteer Ref: 43 C2
Closed: 1965
Shed-Code: 88D (1964-1965)
Allocations: December 1964

Class 56xx 0-6-2T

5601*	5651	5681	6612	6658
5605*	5655	5686*	6622	6661
5618	5659	5688*	6649*	6691
5621	5677	5696	6655	

Total 19

Locos marked (*) are ex-Abercynon 88E. Remainder are engines which transferred from Merthyr 88D upon its closure.

Previously a sub shed to Merthyr 88D, Rhymney became 88D in November 1964 when the former depot closed.

The shed had a short lifetime as a coded depot and closed in April 1965 when the remaining engines transferred to the London Midland Region and Llanelly 87F. A number were placed in store at the shed but they were all withdrawn by June 1965.

The overall scene at Rhymney shed in September 1962 with the coaler just visible behind the water tower. The presence of daylight within the shed provides evidence of roof dilapidation.
W. T. Stubbs

88E ABERCYNON

Origin: GWR (1929)
Gazetteer Ref: 43 C3
Closed: 1964
Shed-Code: 88E (1949-1964)
Allocations: 1950

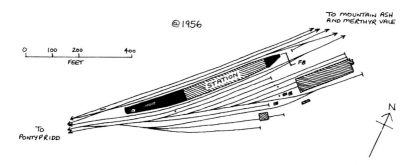

*Abercynon shed in 1962 with Nos 3730 and 5686
(both 88E) occupying the left foreground.*
N. E. Preedy

Class TV 0-6-2T

219	295	337	356	386
236	304	351	380	397

Class 16xx 0-6-0PT
1620

Class 1901 0-6-0PT
2008

Class 54xx 0-6-0PT
5421

Class 56xx 0-6-2T

5618	5637	5644	5686
5619	5641	5650	6661
5630	5643	5682	

Class 64xx 0-6-0PT

6401	6411	6438

Total 27

Allocations: 1959

Class 16xx 0-6-0PT

1610	1620

Class 57xx 0-6-0PT

3707	3734	7726	7744	9622
3730	3783	7733	8735	

Class 56xx 0-6-2T

5601	5623	5643	5682
5617	5627	5644	5686
5618	5641	5680	5699

Class 64xx 0-6-0PT

6435	6438

Total 25

Abercynon closed in November 1964 and the remaining locos transferred to Cardiff Radyr 88B, Rhymney 88D (see Rhymney 1964 allocation) and Neath 87A.

'56xx' 0-6-2T No 6628 (88E) outside Abercynon in October 1964, a month before closure and the locos transfer to Neath 87A.   J. L. Stevenson

88F TREHERBERT

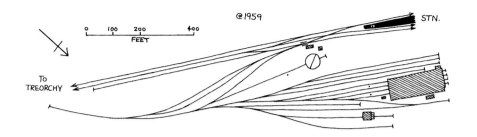

@1959

Origin: GWR (1931)
Gazetteer Ref: 43 D2
Closed: 1965
Shed-Code: 88F (1949-1965)
Allocations: 1950

Class TV 0-6-0T

193	194	195

Class TV 0-6-2T

207	218	290	365	399
210	278	299	366
215	279	303	368
216	285	352	378

Class 51xx 2-6-2T

4162	4177	5159

Class 56xx 0-6-2T

5600	5611	5668	5691	6655
5607	5613	5676	5693
5608	5615	5680	5695
5610	5663	5688	6648

Allocations: 1959

Class 56xx 0-6-2T

5600	5613	5654	5684	5695
5607	5632	5665	5687	6619
5608	5637	5668	5691
5610	5646	5676	5693
5611	5653	5678	5694

Total 22

Treherbert closed in March 1965 and its last four locos transferred to Pontypool Road 86G, Ebbw Junction 86B and Severn Tunnel Junction 86E.

A trio of ex-Taff Vale 0-6-2Ts and a '56xx' 0-6-2T at Treherbert in July 1949. Left to right are 305 (88A), 303, 365 (both 88F) and 5629 (87B).
N. E. Preedy collection

89A OSWESTRY

Pre-Grouping Origin: Cambrian Railways
Gazetteer Ref: 20 G4
Closed: 1965
Shed-Codes: 89A (1949-1960)
89D (1960-1963)
6E (1963-1965)
Allocations: 1950 (89A)

Cambrian Railway 0-6-0

844	855	887	895
849	873	893	896

Class 14xx 0-4-2T

1412	1432	5803	5812
1428	1459	5806	

Class 16xx 0-6-0PT
1604

@ 1951

To STN.

To WHITTINGTON

N

0	100	200	300

FEET

Class 2021 0-6-0PT

2032	2054	2068	2075

Class 2251 0-6-0

2210	2244	2255	3208

Class 2301 0-6-0

2327	2408	2482	2516	2556
2354	2409	2483	2538	2572
2386	2449	2484	2543	

Class 74xx 0-6-0PT

7405	7410	7434

'Manor' 4-6-0
7807 *Compton Manor*
7808 *Cookham Manor*
7819 *Hinton Manor*

Class 81xx 2-6-2T
8103

Class 90xx 4-4-0

9001	9016	9022	9028
9003	9020	9026	

'Duke' 4-4-0
9084 *Isle of Jersey*

Total 53

Allocations: 1959 (89A)

Class 14xx 0-4-2T

1432	1458

Class 16xx 0-6-0PT

1602	1603	1604

Class 2251 0-6-0

2219	2239	2294	3202	3209
2236	2275	3200	3208	

Class 57xx 0-6-0PT

3600	3789	5726	9681

Class 54xx 0-6-0PT

5400	5422

Class 43xx 2-6-0
6342

Class 64xx 0-6-0PT
6404

Class 74xx 0-6-0PT
7405   7410   7434

'Manor' 4-6-0
7800 *Torquay Manor*
7801 *Anthony Manor*
7807 *Compton Manor*
7819 *Hinton Manor*
7822 *Foxcote Manor*
7827 *Lydham Manor*

Class 90xx 4-4-0
9005

Oswestry in 1949 prior to the rebuilding of the roof.
Real Photos

Oswestry from the coaler in June 1961. The loco facing is 'Manor' 4-6-0 No 7810 Draycott Manor *whilst the one nearest the camera is '14xx' 0-4-2T No 1458 (both 89D Oswestry).*   N. E. Preedy

Class 2 2-6-0

46503	46507	46511	46514	46524
46504	46509	46512	46515	46526
46505	46510	46513	46523	46527

Total 47

Oswestry was recoded 89D in October 1960 and latterly 6E when it became part of the London Midland Region in September 1963.

The shed closed in January 1965 when the bulk of its allocation went to Croes Newydd 6C and Shrewsbury 6D.

89B BRECON

Pre-Grouping Origin: Brecon & Merthyr Tydfil Junction Railway
Gazetteer Ref: 14 F3
Closed: 1962
Shed-Codes: 89B (1949-1959)
88K (1961-1962)
Allocations: 1950 (89B)

Class 2251 0-6-0
2287

Class 2301 0-6-0
2343   2351   2401   2452   2468

Class 57xx 0-6-0PT
3638   3706   3767   3770

Class 14xx 0-4-2T
5801

Total 11

Allocations: 1959 (89B)

Class 2251 0-6-0
2225   2287

Class 57xx 0-6-0PT
3638   3706   3767   3770

Class 2 2-6-0
46508   46518   46520   46522
46516   46519   46521

Total 13

Brecon lost its code in November 1959 and became a sub-shed of Oswestry 89A. The allocation was divided between Oswestry 89A and Newport Ebbw Junction 86A.

In January 1961 the depot was afforded the code 88K but did not receive any allocated engines and carried on as before with locos from Oswestry and Ebbw.

On Sunday, 22 April 1962 the following locos were 'on shed': 2218, 2240, 2247, 3691, 3706, 3714 (all 86A), 46507, 46509, 46510, 46521, 46523 (all 89D Oswestry). These engines are likely to have been Brecon's working allocation for this period.

The shed closed in December 1962 (as 88K).

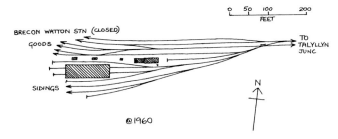

Brecon shed in 1954 with '57xx' 0-6-0PT and '2MT' 2-6-0 classes sharing the metals. Left to right are Nos 3767, 3638, 46518 and 46522 (all 89B).
Photomatic

89C MACHYNLLETH

Pre-Grouping Origin: Cambrian Railways
Gazetteer Ref: 14 B5
Closed: 1966
Shed-Codes: 89C (1949-1963)
6F (1963-1966)
Allocations: 1950 (89C)

Cambrian Railway 0-6-0
864	892	894

Class 14xx 0-4-2T
1465	1474

Class 16xx 0-6-0PT
1603

Class 2251 0-6-0
2200	2206	2260	2298	3202
2201	2219	2283	3200	3207
2204	2223	2292	3201	

Class 2301 0-6-0
2323

Class 45xx 2-6-2T
4501	4549	4571	5507	5541
4512	4555	4575	5517	5560
4530	4560	4581	5524	5570

Class 74xx 0-6-0PT
7406	7417

'Manor' 4-6-0
7802 *Bradley Manor*
7803 *Barcote Manor*

Class 90xx 4-4-0
9000	9005	9013	9021	9027
9002	9009	9014	9024	
9004	9012	9017	9025	

Total 53

Allocations: 1959 (89C)

Class 14xx 0-4-2T
1449	5809

Class 16xx 0-6-0PT
1636

Class 2251 0-6-0
2200	2217	2244	2271	2286
2201	2232	2255	2280	2298
2202	2233	2260	2281	
2204	2237	2264	2285	

Class 45xx 2-6-2T
4549	4575	5553	5565
4560	5541	5556	5570

Class 43xx 2-6-0
6335	6371	6378	6392

Class 74xx 0-6-0PT
7406	7417

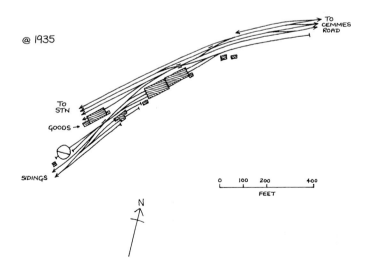

@ 1935

To CEMMES ROAD

To STN

GOODS →

SIDINGS

0 100 200 400
FEET

N

125

'Manor' 4-6-0
7802 *Bradley Manor*
7803 *Barcote Manor*
7806 *Cockington Manor*
7814 *Fringford Manor*

Class 90xx 4-4-0
9015   9017

Class 2 2-6-0
78000   78003   78006
78002   78005   78007

Total 47

Allocations: 1965 (6F)

Class 2251 0-6-0
2236   2268   3208

Class 2MT 2-6-0
46446   46521

Class 4MT 4-6-0
75002   75004

Class 4MT 2-6-4T
80097   80099   80104
80098   80101   80105

Total 13

Machynlleth became London Midland Region property in September 1963 and was recoded 6F. The shed closed in December 1966 with the bulk of its engines finding homes at Shrewsbury 6D and Croes Newydd 6C.

Standard Class 2 2-6-0 No 78007 (89C) outside the eastern end of Machynlleth in July 1961. K. Fairey

List of Shed-Codes

The following list sets out every shed-code that existed for steam Motive Power Depots under the Western Region from 1949 to 1966 along with each venue and its length of occupancy.

81A Old Oak Common 1949-65
81B Slough 1949-64
81C Southall 1949-65
81D Reading 1949-65
81E Didcot 1949-65
81F Oxford 1949-66

82A Bristol Bath Road 1949-60
82B St Philips Marsh 1949-64
82C Swindon 1949-64
82D Westbury 1949-63
82E Yeovil Pen Mill 1949-58
    Bristol Barrow Road 1958-65
82F Weymouth 1949-58
    Bath Green Park 1958-66
82G Templecombe 1958-63

83A Newton Abbot 1949-63
83B Taunton 1949-64
83C Exeter 1949-63
    Westbury 1963-65
83D Plymouth Laira 1949-63
    Exmouth Junction 1963-65
83E St Blazey 1949-62
    Yeovil Town 1963-65
83F Truro 1949-62
    Barnstaple Junction 1963-64
83G Penzance 1949-62
    Templecombe 1963-66
83H Plymouth Friary 1958-63

84A Wolverhampton Stafford Road
      1949-63
    Plymouth Laira 1963-64
84B Wolverhampton Oxley 1949-63
84C Banbury 1949-63
84D Leamington Spa 1949-63
84E Tyseley 1949-63
    Wadebridge 1963-64
84F Stourbridge 1949-63
84G Shrewsbury 1949-60
    Kidderminster 1960-63
84H Wellington 1949-63
84J Croes Newydd 1949-60
84K Chester (GWR) 1949-58
    Wrexham Rhosddu 1958-60

85A Worcester 1949-65
85B Gloucester Horton Road 1949-65
85C Hereford 1949-60
    Gloucester Barnwood 1960-64
85D Kidderminster 1949-60
    Bromsgrove 1960-64
85E Gloucester Barnwood 1958-60
85F Bromsgrove 1958-60

86A Ebbw Junction 1949-63
86B Newport Pill 1949-63
    Ebbw Junction 1963-65
86C Cardiff Canton 1949-60
    Hereford 1960-64

86D Llantrisant 1949-60
86E Severn Tunnel Junction 1949-65
86F Tondu 1949-60
    Aberbeeg 1960-64
86G Pontypool Road 1949-65
86H Aberbeeg 1949-60
86J Aberdare 1949-60
86K Abergavenny 1949-55
    Tredegar 1955-60

87A Neath 1949-65
87B Duffryn Yard 1949-64
87C Danygraig 1949-60
87D Swansea East Dock 1949-64
87E Landore 1949-61
87F Llanelly 1949-65
87G Carmarthen 1949-64
87H Neyland 1949-63
    Whitland 1963
87J Fishguard Goodwick 1949-63
87K Swansea Victoria 1949-59

88A Cardiff Cathays 1949-57
    Cardiff Radyr 1957-60
    Cardiff Canton 1960-62
    Cardiff East Dock 1963-65
88B Cardiff East Dock 1949-58
    Cardiff Radyr 1960-65
88C Barry 1949-64
88D Merthyr 1949-64
    Rhymney 1964-65
88E Abercynon 1949-64
88F Treherbert 1949-65
88G Llantrisant 1960-64
88H Tondu 1960-64
88J Aberdare 1960-65
88K Brecon 1961-62
88L Cardiff East Dock 1962-63

89A Oswestry 1949-60
    Shrewsbury 1960-63
89B Brecon 1949-59
    Croes Newydd 1960-63
89C Machynlleth 1949-63
89D Oswestry 1960-63

Index